CAREER
30 LESSONS
I LEARNT
ALONG THE WAY

BAYO ADEYINKA

30

CAREER
30 LESSONS
I LEARNT ALONG THE WAY

BAYO ADEYINKA

Copyright © 2018 by Bayo Adeyinka

All rights reserved. No part of this publication may be reproduced, distributed, or transmitted in any form or by any means, including photocopying, recording, or other electronic or mechanical methods, without the prior written permission of the publisher or Author (Bayo Adeyinka), except in the case of brief quotations embodied in critical reviews and certain other noncommercial uses permitted by copyright law.

Bayo Adeyinka
email: greaterbayo@gmail.com

CONTENTS

A lengthy dedication for a wonderful woman	8
Acknowledgements	12
Foreword	16
Introduction	17
Lesson 1: Mind Your Language & Other Interview Lessons	19
Lesson 2: No One Gets Paid What They Deserve	24
Lesson 3: Develop Emotional Intelligence	29
Lesson 4: Customers Are More Than Mere Statistics	32
Lesson 5: Learn To Manage Office Politics	36
Lesson 6: Do The Exceptional	40
Lesson 7: Manage Your Superiors	43
Lesson 8: Be Street Smart	46
Lesson 9: Be Tactful	50
Lesson 10: Get A Mentor	53
Lesson 11: Change Jobs The Smart Way	58
Lesson 12: Be Friendly	63

Lesson 13:	Don't Burn Bridges	66
Lesson 14:	Never Chase Money	70
Lesson 15:	Find Problems And Solve Them	72
Lesson 16:	The Best Advice I Received In My Career	75
Lesson 17:	Be Spontaneous. Be Fluid	78
Lesson 18:	Don't Be A One-Role Specialist	80
Lesson 19:	Communication Skills Are Important	82
Lesson 20:	Don't Do It If You Can't Talk About It	87
Lesson 21:	Competence Is Key	91
Lesson 22:	Regularly Set And Update Your Goals	94
Lesson 23:	Future-Proof Your Career	97
Lesson 24:	Have A Plan B	101
Lesson 25:	Don't Point The Gun If you Don't intend to shoot, & Other Great Rules For Supervisors	105
Lesson 26:	Bending The Rules Make You Crooked	109
Lesson 27:	Don't Lose Your Life While Chasing A Career	111
Lesson 28:	Remember To Have Fun At Work	114
Lesson 29:	Your Best Retirement Plans Are The People You Build	117
Lesson 30:	Find Meaning Outside Your Career	120
Personal notes		124

ENDORSEMENTS

Bayo Adeyinka is a man I have admired for years. He is filled with the wisdom and knowledge of God. He has lived his life openly and well and is an inspiration to many people including me. I am so excited for this book *30 Career Lessons I Learnt Along the Way* because contained in the pages of this book are words that have the power to potentially change people's lives forever.

There is no magic formula for a successful career life. It requires a well-thought-out plan of action, focus, patience, perseverance, discipline and a clear-cut objective. This book is for anyone seeking advice on a successful career. Having this book at a time like this is phenomenal as most of the graduates churned out of our higher institutions of learning lack employable skills. Now, they have a reason to take charge of their careers.

-Preye Jimoh
An employee for over 20 years, now MD/CEO of Dove Spa Group (Beauty & Wellness Out t)

The book is a treasure. It deals with soft skills that are usually not taught anywhere. The author's many stories make it very practical and easy to read. You'll not only learn but you'll enjoy it.

-Abayomi Ojumu,
Programme Test Assurance Consultant
Chelsea and Westminster Hospital NHS Foundation, UK

This book is a must-read for all new hires and even experienced ones. So many landmines will be easily navigated if the lessons are held to heart. It's very deep. A recommended text for every hire.

-Olatunde Phillips Ajayi-Ope
CEO Nonesuch House Publishers
(Publisher, Designer, Creative Critique and Content Provider)

Adebayo Adeyinka is a seasoned banker whose versatility about knowledge within and outside his industry has defied all odds. I got particularly interested in him after following him on social media. His style of communication and choice of words are exceptional. His style of objective summary is so unique with imaginary feelings of being present at such events.

He has not just challenged the norms on many occasions especially from his industry perspective. He makes me validate why self-development pays the highest dividend for any individual. As a Human Resources Practitioner, having such a resourceful employee not only makes him an asset to any organisation but to the country at large.

I am happy our paths have crossed once again, even after knowing him for over two decades. His ability to leave good footprints in the minds of many youths of today and to use various media to reach out and impact lives gives me hope about the future in Nigeria. He is not the regular social media writer; he takes actions and ensures something is done.

His selfless nature of giving back to the community has made him organize many professional seminars for the youth with aim of "addressing & closing gaps" from the huge decay in the educational sector which directly affects the outputs to the work force in Nigeria.

He is a prolific writer which is one skill I became his mentee in. He has mastered the skill of oral and written communication perfectly. He is also an excellent time manager, which is one of the greatest skills to being successful.
Alfred & Victoria is glad to partner with you and the platform we have created where people of like minds address some of these myriads of issues pertaining to the Nigerian Workforce.

-Bunmi Teru
Principal Consultant,
Alfred & Victoria Associates

A LENGTHY DEDICATION FOR A WONDERFUL WOMAN

It took me six months of persistence to sign on her account. In that time, I visited her at least twice in a week and for some reason, I kept going. Although she didn't budge, she remained very friendly—much so that I stopped pitching and would just go to say hello. I would simply sit with her and engage in small talk for some minutes. And she always had a bottle of coke on her table that she would graciously offer to me.

One beautiful afternoon, just when I was about giving up, I got a call and she spoke in Yoruba with her characteristic motherly voice: "Bayo, bring your account opening forms right now". I couldn't believe my ears. I ran to her office in a jiffy!

Over the years, we developed a mother-son relationship. Truly, everyone called her mummy but she was a special customer to me. I have never met anyone so kind-hearted. I even had to express my fear that people would take advantage of her kindness but her staff reassured me. To my surprise, her managers had been working with her for more than ten years at the time.

I was even indeed astonished that she had built houses for her staff to reward their commitment. I have not come across more dedicated staff in my career! They were loyal to a fault.

There were at least three times when her intervention was critical to my situation. The first was when I was building my house. As all the funds were coming from my monthly salary, it was a real struggle to keep it going at a steady pace. Still I was determined to plaster the walls before the rains arrived that year.

I kept wondering how long it would take to save enough money, and if I would have to wait until the approaching rainy season would end. Incidentally, selling cement was one of mummy's key businesses and a colleague prodded me to patronize her.

I approached her manager and offered to pay for my requirement in two instalments. He laughed and asked me to see mummy for which I was initially hesitant. As we spoke, she came down the staircase and saw both of us discussing. She expressed surprise that I was visiting but didn't come to her office.

"What are you discussing with manager?" she asked.
It was the manager who then told her my financing request.

"Bayo, what do you need?" she asked.
I opened up to her that I needed 100 bags of cement but I could only afford to split the payment.

She was furious. She asked me to go back to my office because she was going out.

About two hours later, my phone rang and it was her.

"Are you in your office?" she asked.

I responded in the affirmative.

Then she said, "Look outside your window. A trailer is there with 150 bags of cement. I have also put 4 boys to help you offload them. Is your driver around? Tell him to lead them to your site".

I raised my window blinds and saw the truck. My jaw dropped. I explained to her that I needed only 100 bags but she told me there are usually variations and I could use the rest for flooring. I thanked her profusely.

Her response was, "Bayo, Never mind"

I made sure I honoured my commitment to pay in two instalments. I paid back earlier than promised. Months later, after she realised that I had fully paid up, she still asked if it was convenient for me!

Although my career progress was related to a particular decision I took, I wouldn't have been able to make that decision without her help. Successfully managing her account put me under favourable spotlight. My performance helped my branch become the rave of the time. therefore, when the opportunity to move to Lagos came up, my application sailed through easily because of the leverage that her business with our bank gave me. that move redefined my entire career.

When I informed her that I was relocating to Lagos, she was almost in tears.

I sat with her in her office and let her know that her business was one of the reasons I got the upward move to Lagos. I assured her that the person I handed the account over to would maintain the relationship as well. Besides, I would only be a phone call away.

Truly, she kept in touch by phone and even gave me several business referrals in Lagos. that was until she had some challenges in her business. I would try her lines several times but wouldn't be able to connect. On one occasion when I got through and expressed my empathy, she would tell me in her characteristic manner that it was nothing and that she would get over it.

One dreadful day in February, Kóláwolé Fábekú called me to break the sad news: Mrs Modupe Sobodu was dead. She had been struggling with breast cancer and we didn't know. I broke down and wept. Apart from when I lost my younger brother, that is the only other time I cried. It was a personal loss to me. Every time I walk through the doors of my house (which I have since completed) I remember what she did for me. I also remember my career move to Lagos and her contribution to it. I continue to carry her memories in my heart.

I have dedicated this book to late Mrs Modupe Sobodu, a kind-hearted customer whose influence remains alive even though she's now with the saints triumphant. I am indebted to you.

ACKNOWLEDGEMENTS

Over the course of my career, I've been blessed to come across several people who have contributed at one time or the other in making me the person I am today.

I am forever thankful to Mr Kayode Fasola, my first branch manager. I was a rookie but he didn't make me feel like one. He was the first person to spot my sales potentials and I learnt a lot from him (especially humility) by following him on calls.

Mr Victor Odunjo took me under his wings and helped me to address issues beyond work. His life influenced me greatly. I still recall that both of us were usually the last to close at work and he would drop me on off my way home. Those moments I spent riding with him were priceless.

Mr Oyeyinka Oyelakin was my first line manager. Apart from learning the rudiments of banking, I learnt how to handle subordinates from him. He was a hands-on boss who would join you to perform your tasks. He was so amiable that he allowed me to drive his car. Around the time we started work, my mum fell seriously ill and it was he who personally drove the car to convey her to the hospital.

Mr Bode Abikoye taught me how to write. He made me pen down memos and would spend time correcting them until I rewrote them perfectly. He encouraged me to go after knowledge and be better than the rest. I had the privilege of working with him in three different organizations and he was instrumental to giving me a lead to the international bank I worked for.

Mr Bunmi Atobiloye remains one of the most outstanding bosses I've had. He was a strong believer in my capacity and gave me so many opportunities to demonstrate my potential. There was a time an anonymous person wrote to the Managing Director, complaining about me. It was Mr Atobiloye who stood by me, insisting the petitioner was wrong and vouching for my integrity. I can never forget that episode.

Aramide Ajayi stunned me during my first presentation as a branch manager. After everyone clapped for what I thought was a brilliant presentation, she dissented and tore it apart. I was initially mortified until she finished speaking. She told everyone that she knows me and that what I presented was below my potential. Indeed, she helped me rise above mediocrity and to gun for excellence. She looks tough but has a heart of gold. She's a motivator per excellence. She's one person that when she asks me to jump, my response will be, 'How high?'

Titi Olarinde helped give my career a quantum leap. She gave me a lot of opportunities and was an incredible believer in my abilities. She has a unique ability to identify talents and to deploy them to their area of strengths. She related with me like a younger brother and I told not a few people that she could never hurt me as I've forgiven her in advance.

Nneka Onyeali-Ikpe brought out a side in me that I never knew existed. Working with her made me mature and strong in my convictions. She is never sentimental about issues and I learnt objectivity from her. Our paths have crossed thrice and each time she's been my direct supervisor. Twice, I have benefited from her benevolence. She's a relentless goal-getter who can squeeze water from a stone.

Ola Olabinjo came to my rescue at a very critical time in my career. Though I worked with him just for a short period, I can never forget his impact on my professional life. His objectivity, drive and candour are second to none.

Mr Gbenga Apampa whose guidance over the years have become invaluable and whose insights and reviews of this book are most treasured.

I have also worked with several colleagues who made life easier for me and work more interesting:

Folaranmi Jemirin, still one of the best staff I've worked with. Suave, amiable and highly professional, he was extremely loyal. I never had to micro-manage him. I'm yet to see a staff like him who consistently gives beyond 100% to every task.

Ijeoma Nwachukwu, a dear colleague who helped me navigate my way during very turbulent times. She's an encourager. We became very close friends and she's like a sister to me now.

Oji Ijere, who gave a recommendation on my behalf that landed me a good career move. We worked together in two different organizations.

Eze Nwakanma, an absolute gentleman who gave me wise counsel at a time I was in dire straits. He is fiercely loyal and highly cerebral. We worked together in two different organizations and he's one person I'll be willing to work with every time.

Lovette Pogu, a dedicated goal-getter and workaholic. She sniffs opportunities from a distance. She's truly dependable. We worked together for two organizations.

Chetachi Ezenagu, a wonderful colleague who inspires me with her life and dedication to work. If you're looking for someone who will not take no for an answer, that's Cheta— as we call her. We've worked together at three organizations.

Dr Olatunde Asagba, my wonderful editor who soaked in my pressure to turn out an outstanding job. She edited my previous book and also voiced half of the audio book. It's simply amazing knowing she's a dentist with multiple caps.

I can't forget my wife, Abimbola who gave me wings to fly. She has never complained in spite of my usually busy schedule and she encourages me to maximize my career. there have been many phone calls from her (sometimes deep into the night) sharing tips on what to do in many tight situations. Her advice has been invaluable to me. If anyone deems me successful, due credit should go to her.

To all these people and many more, I'm sincerely grateful.

FOREWORD

If your aspiration as a young man or woman is to achieve more than the average in life, then this book provides just the right tips. As a career and growth consultant in Africa and Europe since 2005, I have not read a more practical book that addresses key gaps in career development, especially for young people.

This book drops nuggets right from the first lesson which addresses interview techniques through a compilation of the writer's real life encounters with some African graduate job seekers; through to the fourth lesson which exposes the reader to the benefits of customer service, the lack of which is a major draw-back to most African businesses; and the fifteenth lesson which reveals the solving of problems as the key to rapid career elevation.

The twenty-ninth lesson encourages an appetite in helping others build their lives as an investment in one's own retirement plan. I was particularly drawn to this lesson as I build people for a living and now I see I am in fact investing in my retirement. A practical and enjoyable piece.

Benjamin O. Taiwo
Business & Employability Strategist
Ahead Strategies, UK.

INTRODUCTION

I started my career without having any guidance. I was a graduate of mechanical engineering, thus banking was unfamiliar territory for me.
I didn't know what to expect. Neither did I know how to navigate through the various issues and avoid those landmines that would dot the landscape of my career. Nobody taught me how to handle work relationships or supervisors while in school. I was also not taught the soft skills required to make my career interesting.

I've also come across so many people who are confused about their careers. Some are stuck between different options. This book is my attempt to deal with a number of such career issues. I share my experience across about seven financial institutions, spanning almost twenty years.

But it doesn't matter what your field is—banking, teaching, law, accounting, agriculture, IT—or even if you're just starting to prepare for your career. this book is a good resource that will answer a lot of questions and brighten your steps.

1

LESSON ONE

MIND YOUR LANGUAGE & OTHER INTERVIEW LESSONS*

> *Your appearance is what we see first before we hear what you have to say.*

Each time I conduct interviews, I usually end up shaking my head and lamenting the state of education in Nigeria. Our tertiary institutions are churning out graduates who are mostly unemployable. On a particular day, I interviewed near 50 candidates and by the end of the whole session, my only conclusion was that we have a BIG

problem.

In one particular instance, I was alarmed when I perused the CV of a lady, a graduate of one of the universities in the Southwest. It was full of outlandish errors, so I asked her to spell a few words. She spelt the word 'redeemed' wrongly four times before she got it right on the fifth try. Meanwhile, she had described herself as one of the officials of the Redeemed Christian

Fellowship while she was an undergraduate.

She couldn't spell the word 'corper' after five aempts. Yet she had taught pupils at a school during her national service. I underlined about 10 grammatical errors on her CV and showed them to her. She couldn't even determine where to use the apostrophe 's'.

One candidate couldn't construct a whole sentence correctly. Even when I repeated the errors, hoping that he would correct himself, he was clueless. Another candidate found it difficult explaining what he studied in school.

Also, there are some who have not developed themselves in any way since they graduated. I had to spend some time to talk to a lady who had obtained her Ordinary National Diploma (OND) fifteen years ago but had not done anything to improve upon herself since then. When she mentioned the issue of paucity of funds, I pointed at her designer bag and her well braided hair as evidence that it was not the problem.

I asked a female candidate what her aspirations would be, if money was not a restraining factor. Her answer le all of us on the interview panel with mouths wide open.

"I want to live large and live big", was what she said.

Another candidate told us he studied 'BSc Economics'. He made the mistake thrice until I informed him that he studied economics and not BSc Economics. A fellow was asked to introduce himself and he started with "My names are..." I had to ask him how many people he was introducing. Even when I tried to correct him, he insisted that he was right so I had to give up.

A few guys—at least three of them that I recall—had the labels of their suit on their sleeves. When I asked why the labels were not removed, they grinned sheepishly. One of them told me that is the current trend. When that same guy sat down, I observed that he wore ankle socks with a significant part of his lower legs showing bare skin.

One candidate was particularly striking for his naivety. He came in shaking and stammered while introducing himself. He could barely string a sentence together. When I tried to make him comfortable by asking him to take a deep breath, he answered by saying, "I don't know why I'm like this today. This is actually my first interview". He had just finished his national service and anxiety was written all over him.

I made two major observations during the interview session that day*:

1. Candidates who engaged in extracurricular activities while in school interviewed better. There was a lady who was a member of SIFE (Students in Free Enterprise) while she was on campus and she was one of the bright spots of the day. There was another fellow who had represented his university at a competition outside Nigeria. He was also outstanding. Likewise, a lady who was vice president of her students' union while she was an undergraduate demonstrated a lot of confidence during the interview.

2. Candidates who attended private universities in Nigeria generally performed better. There must be something that those schools are getting right as their graduates communicated better and demonstrated a far more superior level of intelligence. I was disappointed by the performance of most graduates of mainstream universities and polytechnics. One could almost guess whether a candidate attended a private university just by

listening to them.

If you're preparing for an interview, it's in your best interest to do some research about the company you want to work with. Google is your friend. Also, work on your communication skills. You should be able to talk about yourself very clearly and also describe what you have done before, if you're an experienced hire.

Your body language is critical. Do not fidget or show your anxiety. We all have butterflies in our stomach when we face strange people on an interview panel but with a smile on your face, no one should ever know. A lady cracked her knuckles throughout the interview today. It was a tad irritating. Also, your posture is important. Don't slouch on the chair. Sit straight with your back on the chair, and your legs together.

Mind your language while being interviewed. It's better to be brief than to be unnecessarily verbose. By talking too much at times, you demonstrate that you know so little. Pronounce words well. It can take some practice but stand in front of a mirror and rehearse until you get better. Be ready to defend your qualifications. Demonstrate that you actually earned your degree. Maintain eye contact. That shows your level of confidence.

Also, good grooming is key. No matter the current fad, it's safer to be conservative in your dressing. Dark coloured outfits are best for interviews. Stay with white or blue shirts for men. You can never go wrong with them. You must have a great sense of colour to want to try very bright colours. It's either it turns out so good or you turn out like a magician's apprentice.

Ladies have the latitude to try out more colours but the simpler, the better. Pay attention to your hair and hand bag and the makeup should be light.

Match your colours properly. Avoid loud jewellery. Look your best as the book is open judged by the cover during interviews. Your appearance is what we see first before we hear what you have to say.

We need to declare a state of emergency in our education sector and even start to teach intending graduates certain life skills. Nigerian graduates will not be able to compete with their African counterparts in a few years at this rate.

*Culled from an article I wrote on March 15, 2018 called The Interview. The article was shared over 4,000 times on Facebook alone and published by some newspapers.

LESSON TWO

NO ONE GETS PAID WHAT THEY DESERVE

> "Let us never negotiate out of fear. But let us never fear to negotiate"
> - *John F. Kennedy*

The first offer might not be the best offer. I learnt this lesson in 2007, when I had completed a series of interviews with a prospective employer. First, I had sat for an aptitude test and faced a panel interview. These were followed by several phone discussions and I was finally offered a salary.

Truth be told, I would have worked for next to nothing at that organization because it was my dream job. Just the name of the bank on my resume would paint my profile in an exquisite colour. It was a once-in-a-lifetime opportunity for me.

This was why the first offer that the HR lady made to me over the phone was attractive. It was better than what I was being paid at the time and I almost jumped at it. For some reason, however, I decided to negotiate. I told her that I already espoused the value that the new organization needed and ought to be paid based on that. We went back and forth for the next three days. Eventually, the pay was significantly increased and I accepted the offer.

It was when I resumed at the new place of work that I discovered that there were many people on the same level earning different salaries. there were even some junior officers who earned more than their hierarchy. In short, the pay was based on the ability to negotiate.

But this is not only limited to salary. In 2002, I was interviewed by a panel which consisted of the managing director of the organization (an Indian national), an executive director, a general manager and the head of human resources. As a new branch of the bank was about to open in Ibadan, so many candidates were interviewed on that day.

I was being interviewed for a sales role and when asked for the grade level that I wanted, I mentioned a step higher than what I should have asked for. Now, prior to this, I only had about two years of banking experience. Also, because some part of this period was spent in operations/back office, I had not been involved in sales for more than a year.

I recall that the executive director almost sent me out of the room because of my audacity but the managing director intervened. The role I asked for was one that would ordinarily take people about five years from entry level with consistent promotion to get to and it was two steps higher than my grade at the time!

When I was asked why I insisted on the role, I spoke about the value that I would bring. I told them that I knew Ibadan like the back of my hand and that I had key contacts which could impact our business development. I still remember the look on the face of the managing director when he told me that he would ask for the last time if I would be willing to take a lower offer.

I was about to change my mind at this point; after all, accepting it would still have been a promotion for me. However, before I could say anything, the general manager stretched his leg under the oval table and pressed my left foot very firmly. As I winced in pain, I looked at him and saw him slightly shake his head. It was a pointer that I should not budge. So with a smile on my face, I respectfully rejected the offer and insisted humbly that getting my preferred offer would be a major motivation to work hard.

Just like that, the MD waved away the executive director who had just declared that the interview was over. He then went on to tell me that he would give me what I wanted but I should be ready to roll up my sleeves and work as he would not hesitate to hire me if I fell short of my sales commitment. All the candidates in the waiting room crowded around me when I got out. They couldn't understand why I was with the panel for an hour when others spent barely ten minutes.

I have seen this scenario play out a couple of times in my career. No one gets paid what they deserve; they get paid what they negotiate. You must therefore hone your negotiation skills. During an interview process, always have the amount that you want to earn at the back of your mind. Otherwise, you will be at the mercy of the interviewer.

You must have done your research on the pay structure of the organization and compare with the industry so you're better prepared. Once you get to the level where you are asked what you want to earn, feel free to offer a figure. I personally think it is unwise to tell the interviewer that they should pay you based on their pay structure, especially when you're an experienced hire.

The fact is that many people are afraid to negotiate. You can conquer that fear by understanding what you are bringing to the table. Be able to communicate this value in vivid terms. Break it down in such a way that the interviewer will understand that you are the indisputable candidate for the role.

In my own case, I was able to demonstrate how I would achieve certain levels of profitability within a period. I spoke about my plans and I highlighted key steps that I would take when employed. I also listed my accomplishments and awards, which were verifiable. The negotiation table is a good place to value yourself without coming off as haughty or arrogant. You need to talk about what you have done and what you will do.

During negotiation, focus on your skills and abilities. Speak about the quick wins. Don't be afraid to say no because most negotiations don't start until someone refuses an offer. Be polite but be firm. Remember to display evident courtesy else your firmness can be interpreted as haughtiness or arrogance. Don't be afraid to ask questions. For instance, are there other perks and benefits apart from the salary?

Throughout the whole process, keep on expressing optimism about the role you're being considered for. Let the interviewer know that you would like to assume that role. Make it clear that you're available. But don't tell lies as this could be a grave error when background checks reveal otherwise. Never tell a lie in order to get a job.

Also, you should never issue ultimatums. You may think that you're the best for that role but there are others who can equally do what you claim to be able to do. Be likeable. Switch on your charm and be at your best. You are most likely to succeed if the interviewer likes you. Negotiation is about influencing decisions, so try to influence the interviewer.

But however hard you may negotiate, you must also show flexibility. Can you actually see that they have constraints? Can you consider the whole deal and not just the salary? Don't have a closed mind when negotiating.

Finally, negotiation is an art which takes time and practice to master. The more you do it, the better you become at it.

LESSON THREE

DEVELOP EMOTIONAL INTELLIGENCE

> "75 percent of careers are derailed for reasons related to emotional competencies, including inability to handle interpersonal problems; unsatisfactory team leadership during times of difficulty or conflict; or inability to adapt to change or elicit trust"
>
> **-Centre for Creative Leadership.**

I've seen very smart people whose careers didn't take off as expected or that got truncated along the way. They had brain power and were obviously smarter than so many of their colleagues but somewhere along the way, they dropped off or didn't get promoted as they should.

Having a high intelligence quotient is not a guarantee for career success and being smart has its limits. You can start to climb your career ladder with a strong IQ but it's a higher dose of emotional intelligence that will sustain you and make you go far.

Emotional intelligence is your ability to understand and recognize emotions in yourself and others, and to use this understanding to manage behaviours, perceptions and relationships. At a certain level in your career, it is no longer about what you know but how you handle yourself and others.

It is your duty to study and to understand the emotions of those whom you work with. I once told a protégé that no matter how aggressive and focused she was on her goals, not developing emotional intelligence would cost her a lot.

There was this lady on my team when I was a branch manager of a commercial bank. She had the best qualification in the team. She was already a chartered accountant at a relatively young age. She was a goal getter, who was very passionate and hungry to deliver on set goals, thus she always met her targets. She was clearly driven and self-motivated. She also got more results than any other member of the team.

She however found it extremely difficult to get along with anyone. I had to settle quarrels between her and others almost on a weekly basis. No one seemed to like her; everyone barely tolerated her. She had no friend at work. We worked in teams, but she worked better alone. It was quite apparent why no one had anything good to say about her when I just resumed at the branch. Even the outgoing branch manager rated her as the weakest link in the team. However, I got along with her because I understood her nature and I had my eyes on the bigger picture, which was the overall effectiveness of the team.

This lady always scored very high on her key performance indicators. Using the Likert scale of 1 to 5 with 1 being the highest and 5 being the lowest, her lowest score when she was on my team was 2. However, on the qualitative ranking which measured so skills such as interpersonal relationships and team work among others, she always scored the lowest. Sadly, she was unable to fully actualize her potential and le the bank.

Be careful how you discuss others at work. Show empathy and don't rush to judge. Don't ever react to any issue in anger. Remember that anger is never a strategy. Don't send mails when you're upset. You can 'draft' the email to express yourself, take a walk or do something else to dissipate your anger. By the time you get back to your 'draft' mail, you will realize the tone of your mail communicates anger and not the information intended, which may negatively impact several things.

Therefore, exercise restraint, even when under immense pressure. Some people will say that they don't take nonsense and that's why they have a short fuse. Well, if you will attain the heights of your career, be ready to take a lot of nonsense along the way.

Be humble and defer to your superiors. You may think that you know more than them but having a haughty attitude will soon show you to the door. You also need to understand that there is a wide gulf between knowledge and experience. You may have the knowledge but it is your willingness to learn and to submit yourself to leadership discipline that will help you garner the required experience to climb the ladder of your career.

4

LESSON FOUR

CUSTOMERS ARE MORE THAN MERE STATISTICS

> "Every person you meet is a potential door to a new opportunity- personally or professionally. Build good bridges even in that just-for now job because you never know how they'll weave into the larger picture of your life"
>
> **- Kristina Leonardi, Career Coach.**

I saw her limp into the banking hall. Her leg was in a cast and she was using crutches. I didn't know when I left all I was doing, went around my enclosure and ran into the banking hall towards her. I knelt and gently touched the bad leg, asking her what had gone wrong. She said that she had broken the leg when she slipped in her bath. Her visit to the bank was however to raise drafts for her children's school fees. I asked her to sit down and rushed back to get a form for her.

At the time, I was the funds transfer officer and one of my core functions was issuing manager's cheques and drafts. I was therefore able to save her the trouble of coming around to my work space. Within minutes, I was done with her request and immediately saw her off to her vehicle.

A few months after that incident, I made the transition from operations to sales in the same bank. Just as I settled into my new role, I got an offer from another bank and was posted to their new branch as a sales staff. On my first day of work, I decided to go out and visit some known names so that I could pitch to them.

As I got to the popular Magazine Road in Jericho, I spotted the car of the woman I described earlier. I asked my driver to catch her attention by flashing the headlamps. When we didn't succeed, I asked him to follow the car and possibly flag her down so I could talk to her. The truth was I didn't know her office or home and I was just lucky to have seen her on the road. Don't forget that my interactions with her had been limited to attending to her requests within the banking space.

Finally, my driver caught up with her and upon seeing me, she pulled off the road. I went to meet her. After exchanging pleasantries, I informed her that I had moved on to another bank. She let out a slight scream and immediately said she would transfer all her funds to my new bank. Right away she went to my former bank and demanded for all her funds in one single draft, which she handed over to me. I took it to my new branch, where it was used to open the very first account in that location!

She told me that she could never forget that incident when I had touched her leg. I didn't know that when I touched her leg, I actually touched her heart.

Around the year 2009, I had a contract staff who worked with me at Apapa,

Lagos. He was simply outstanding in the way he managed customers. He worked with such zeal and energy that not many people knew he wasn't a core staff. In spite of his status, I assigned some valuable customers to him and he never disappointed. He had a way of making customers feel so valued.

One day, one of the high net worth clients he managed called me on the phone. To my surprise, he told me that he just learnt that the man managing his relationship was a contract staff and he was impressed by the outstanding service he received every time. He told me point blank that since my organization did not value such a staff, he would be hiring the lad himself.

This man's office was close to ours. He was the managing director of a leading indigenous oil and gas company in Nigeria. Well, that was how my former staff was hired. Within a few months, he had gone for an offshore training and was given a car, something he had not been able to get for years at our organization.

Anyone who wants to succeed in their career must treat customers as more than statistics. You have to show them that you care. You have to value and appreciate them. Let them know truly that your career depends on them.

Love your customers genuinely. Be interested in them and not just in what they have to offer. There are various ways you can show that you value your customers: know their birthdays, pronounce their names right, visit them when they celebrate or when they are bereaved, send them 'thank you' notes, or hold the door for them.

Little or seemingly insignificant things go a long way to bolster a fledgling career. Like Theodore Roosevelt said, 'people don't really care how much you know until they know how much you care'.

5

LESSON FIVE

LEARN TO MANAGE OFFICE POLITICS

"Always remember that the toes you step on today could be attached to the ass you have to kiss tomorrow"
- Author unknown

Office politics is real, and it happens everywhere. It has the tendency to tear apart even the greatest team. It has ruined otherwise bright and promising careers. It also has the ability to promote careers, if managed effectively.

This is why office politics must be handled in a delicate manner. Don't get involved when superiors are having a tussle. Stay out of it totally (as much as possible). Be neutral. It's safer not to be identified with any camp at all than to be identified with the wrong camp. The wrong camp in this wise is the one that loses out.

Never put yourself in a situation where your statements can be misconstrued. Don't lead a battle if you're not prepared to become a casualty of war. Remember that your silence can never be misquoted.

Some years ago, I worked for a very outstanding financial organization where I got caught up in the bickering among two brilliant superiors to whom I reported. On a particular day, one of them invited me to give a negative testimony about the other to our management team who had come from outside Nigeria. I was asked several leading questions but because I knew the intent, I was very careful with my responses. Eventually, she put me in her bad books and the situation became an albatross.

I have experienced several situations where I was maligned. As human beings, one will get offended but get over it quickly. Understand that the higher you rise in your career, the more you'll be the subject of gossip. Your life will be under scrutiny, so you have to deal as transparently as possible.

There are times when you might not be able to stay neutral for long. At this stage, you need to engage emotional intelligence. The higher you rise in your career, the more politically savvy you must be. An inability to read the tea leaves correctly can spell doom and cut short an otherwise brilliant career.

So when you get into a new organization, watch out for the formal and informal leaders. Informal leaders are the ones who actually dictate how the organization runs, even though they may not have the real titles and authority of the formal leaders. Working with the informal leaders may well be the difference between mere survival and getting ahead in the organization. Know who the real decision makers are.

Next, you need to understand that achieving set targets and your key performance indicators is just half of the job and being talented is certainly not enough. You must be able to develop an effective communication system with your colleagues and superiors.

When you have a clash with people at work, be able to make up easily. Don't wear your emotions on your sleeves. Be careful what you say, write down or send out by mail, especially when angry. Sometimes it's better to just act dumb. Acting dumb doesn't mean you're stupid. Just know when to keep your mouth shut.

I usually tell people that the true promotion list is not the one discussed in the office; rather it is agreed across a table after work, and over a few bottles of drinks. e truth is that people who get promoted often aren't the most qualified. In fact, some careers have been dented by the negative remarks made by a colleague to a superior during lunch.

This is why you must develop and deploy your social and political capital. You may need to speak the right words to those you have identified as having the ears of top management. Mind your speech when you're with office power brokers. Your words have wings and will be amplified.

Every office has its own culture. Understand the culture of the place where you work. And be quick to adapt when there is a change, especially in leadership. With a change in leadership, the rules usually change. Each new leader often tries to form their own power base or structure, so you need to quickly adjust.

Be good at reading people, especially your superiors. Understand their moods. Be sensitive to their body language. Timing is crucial especially if you're seeking a favour. Always give credit to your boss, especially in front of their own superiors, even for things they don't have any input to. Demonstrate loyalty to your boss. Every leader appreciates loyalty.

Apart from this, be in the good books of the immediate staff of your boss, if any. They are good sources of office intelligence and they can give you first-hand information about goings-on. Ignorance is usually not bliss! You need to cultivate these relationships by being nice to them. A card or compliments on their birthdays or special occasions will go a long way. They will fast-track your requests and give you a leverage that others won't get. The same applies to the immediate staff of other superiors in your organization. Don't joke with them.

Competition is fierce and that's why it's a dog-eat-dog situation. There are so many people in the organization and often, so very few slots for a promotion or raise. What then do you do when you're on the same level with many colleagues and the opportunity for a raise is limited to a few slots? You need to compete without appearing to do so. When you're not seen as competition, people tend to ignore or under-rate you. Be opaque. Your rivals shouldn't be able to see through you. Don't display your ambition openly.

A final quick tip about surviving office politics is to develop other abilities that make you relevant and indispensable at work. It may be in the form of so skills such as the ability to organize a party, volunteer on 'special projects' outside your department or a cross functional initiative. In such cases, you become the go to person for that organization and your continuous relevance is guaranteed.

6

LESSON SIX

DO THE EXCEPTIONAL

> *"The world won't be loyal and burden itself to those who are having one skill and talent any longer. Make yourself useful and indispensable".*
> **- Assegid Habtewold, 9 Cardinal Building Blocks: For Continued Success in Leadership**

Here is the truth: no one is indispensable. Still, you can make yourself something close to that. In a very challenging professional environment, your continued relevance depends on how valued you are to the organization. The more valued you become,
the more indispensable you are. People who are important to the goals and aspirations of an organization are not easily disposed of.

One way to remain relevant is to ensure that you are versatile. Have the ability to do more than one thing. When I started my career, I was part of the operations team and my job role was settlements Officer. It was my duty to handle all clearing cheques for my branch and I would have to go to the clearing house. I was also one of the cash movement officers. In addition to these, I managed the server for the branch and handled all low-key technology issues. I was everywhere and everyone needed me at one time or the other.

I still recall a certain day when I took ill and was placed on observation. That day, the branch couldn't open to customers because I was the one who knew the password to the server. My supervisor had to send a vehicle to convey me from the clinic to the branch and back again. It was as if the office couldn't run without me. I was usually the last to close, so I ended up holding unto the keys. And as you may have guessed, I was also the first to arrive at work.

Obviously, your case does not have to be this dramatic. Just ensure that you are versatile and that you do more than is expected of you. Be known for quality work. Be ready to go the extra mile.

I assist my bosses in preparing the slides for their presentations. I also volunteer to do tasks that others are unwilling to do. there was an instance when a branch manager was to go on a vacation and the search for a relieving manager began. No one wanted the job because the location was notorious for its non-performance. I took up the challenge and did my best for those thirty days.

If your supervisor doesn't need to always micromanage you then they will be able to depend on you. Any time we had a stretch budget in one of my former places of employ, I was always willing to take on more than others. I made the work of my supervisors easier as they never needed to bother about me. I accepted whatever I was given and always did my best to meet the set targets.

Be involved in critical areas in the organization. In one company, I was on several committees and made significant contributions.

Be known for deep, introspective thoughts, and workable ideas. Be known as a solution provider. Don't just be a critic or analyst—anyone can do that! However, no matter how valuable you become, understand that no one is truly indispensable. Let that thinking moderate your approach.

7

LESSON SEVEN

MANAGE YOUR SUPERIORS

> *"Servants, obey your boss. Respect him with all your heart..."*
> *- Ephesians 6:4 The Bible (Worldwide English Version)*

One chapter that I dwelled on so much when I read *The 48 Laws of Power* was 'never outshine the master'. This has been my guiding ethos till this day. I believe that it is my duty to make my boss look good and enable them do their job. If my boss fails, then I have failed. So I do everything within my power to ensure that they succeed.

When celebrating a success or achievement, I usually dedicate such to my bosses (no matter how small their input). A win for me is a win for the boss. That way, I have always had a great relationship with all my superiors and in turn, they trust me without reservation.

Your boss deserves 100% loyalty. Anything less is disloyalty. Let your boss know that you have his back covered and do so. Note that loyalty is definitely not the same as sucking up to your boss. Except they don't want to say it out, most bosses know when you're bootlicking. So be genuine and be real. Be trustworthy.

If your boss has to keep looking over their shoulder all the time, then you would soon be made redundant. Make your boss comfortable with you. That's your responsibility. The greatest element in any relationship is trust. Never violate it. If you are privy to confidential information through your boss, then let it remain confidential.

Show understanding when hard decisions are taken. Don't join others to gossip about your superior. e truth is that they will hear everything that was said anyway, so why put yourself at risk? Recognize the moods of your superiors and their styles. Understanding them will help you to navigate your relationship well.

Anticipate the needs of your boss. When you're able to second guess them over a period, you would establish your dependability. Always be a problem solver. Your boss has enough problems already. Be willing to go the extra mile and take on additional responsibilities. Be willing to always take personal responsibility even when you fail. Don't shift the blame to others and never make excuses. Excuses are the easiest thing to make.

Let your boss know that you're available. Years back, as a junior officer, I never leave the office before my boss. Even though I was an entry level staff, he was the one who dropped me off at home because I would stay with him until he closed. And since I held the office keys, I was also the first staff to get to work.

Always carry your boss along. Give them updates frequently, even when not required. That helps to maintain their self-esteem. Always defer to your boss and never argue with them publicly. Consistently put forward a very strong performance because no good manager loathes an excellent staff.

There was a year that my line manager called me into her office and handed a big envelope to me. When I opened it, I found a substantial amount of money that she gave me out of her own bonus and she thanked me for my absolute dedication. I was shocked because I was paid my own bonus and was not expecting her to give me anything.

But no matter how close you think you have become, don't get too familiar with your boss. Always set boundaries. In this way, you will maintain your respect. It's actually very easy to cross the boundaries, especially when you have worked with that superior for a long time. This is why you must remain on your guard.

LESSON EIGHT

BE STREET SMART†

> "You learn how to be book smart in school but you better not forget that you also need to be street smart"
> **-Harvey Mackay**

This chapter comes with a caveat. Don't try this if you're not sure of yourself. It was an appointment that had been scheduled for quite some time. Our regional director was coming into town to meet with the chief medical director (CMD) of a major health establishment. Indeed, we had pitched for a relationship between our bank and them for a while and securing it was going to mark a huge turning point for our branch.

We had already been informed that it was only during this meeting that commitments, if any, would be made. It was such a sensitive stage and each of us was waiting with bated breath. Unfortunately, on the day of the appointment, something came up and our regional director could no longer make the trip.

It was devastating news. This would mean that all our efforts to bring in this deal would come to nought. A representative of the health facility had contacted us about twenty-four hours earlier to confirm the appointment and we could only imagine what their level of disappointment would be if we had to give excuses. Moreover, all the heads of various units were going to accompany the CMD. We certainly could not afford to cancel or reschedule the appointment as it could mean losing the deal to competition. The stakes were high and the implications were massive.

We were still debating on what to do a few hours before the meeting, when my branch manager suddenly exclaimed. He had come up with a brilliant idea. He pointed at me and shouted, "Bayo, you're the regional director".

I didn't understand. At the time, I was just a profit centre manager at the time (a fancy term for team lead in that bank).

"Yes, you will act as our regional director. You have the look, the carriage, and the physical size. Plus they don't know you, unlike me who has been the one relating with them", he concluded.

I rolled my eyes and swallowed hard. I felt sweat drop off my brows. It sounded like a good idea but what if it didn't work? I'd never been a regional director before and I didn't know how to speak like one. What if we were found out for impersonation? So many questions went through my mind.

My branch manager explained his idea. I wasn't to speak so much—after all bosses speak very little. There were different people who would make their own presentations. I was just to say that we appreciate the other establishment for their time and give them our commitment to partner with them and that would be all. I agreed to go ahead with the idea. At least, I thought, I get to be regional director for a few hours.

We lined up a convoy of about five cars. I got into my branch manager's vehicle and sat at the back as we drove to the scheduled meeting place. When we arrived, they were waiting. My branch manager rushed to open the door for me. As I stepped out, I stretched out my arms and he quickly gave me my jacket.

I shook hands with the members of the team, introducing myself as the regional director. I finally took the hands of the chief medical director of the organization and complimented him and his team for the great job being done.

We went into the board room for the meeting where I sat with the CMD. As my team made their presentations, I interjected occasionally with phrases, giving timelines and commitments. I must have acted the part very well because we got the deal on the spot. In addition, we got a space to locate our branch within their premises.

We shook hands and they saw me off to the car. then, the CMD asked for my business card. I almost fainted. I put my hands in my jacket and fumbled around through my pockets. I finally told him that I didn't have any on me and must have forgotten them when rushing down for the meeting. I promised to send one through the branch manager.

As we left the premises, my branch manager gave me a friendly knock on my head. He had referred to me as 'sir' throughout the meeting. Cut a long story short, we got the deal.

Let me share another instance where I had to turn on my street credibility. I had published my first book in conjunction with a friend and was looking for a way for the largest bookstore in Lagos to sell on my behalf. But I had a problem: I was an unknown author and all my emails to the store got no response. So I came up with a plan.

I asked one of my colleagues to visit the bookstore and ask for the book. He did and you can easily predict their response: of course, they had neither heard of the book title nor the author. the next day, I sent another colleague who went through the same motions. About two hours after, I sent my driver who not only visited but went with a copy of the book.

This time around, the bookseller collected the book and remarked that there had been enquiries for the past few days. He wanted to know how he could contact the author. That very evening, I sent another email introducing the book to the store. In less than an hour, I got a response. They wanted to have twenty copies. at was how the bookstore stocked up my book.

Be street smart. Have the ability to be able to think on your feet. There are certain things that you won't learn within the four walls of a university and being street smart is one of them. Being book smart may land you a new job or role but being street smart will help you navigate very difficult situations. It comes with experience on the job.

Being street smart at work demands guts and the truth is that it can go wrong. If it does, be ready to bite the bullet, learn from the mistakes and move on but if it goes right like it did in the stories I just shared, you may get the credit.

9

LESSON NINE

BE TACTFUL

"Step with care and great tact and remember that life's a great balancing act"
- Dr Seuss

I wasn't expecting the email, but when I got it, I was caught between two conflicting emotions. I was happy and confused at the same time. I was happy because my goal of switching from a back office role to sales had been achieved. I was confused because the head of HR wanted me to choose the manager I would be rather work with and they were both copied in the mail. The first one was in charge of the branch where I was while the other was from a location from another state.

While contemplating my line of action, my mobile phone rang. It was the other branch manager. He had read the mail and wanted to find out what my choice would be. He informed me that he was the one who initiated the move to redeploy me to sales and I knew that it was true. He said that a move to work with him would help my career, especially as his branch (although upcountry) was in my state of origin.

I decided to apply tact. Here was a man who had helped my career in several ways versus my own branch manager. I didn't want to offend anyone. So I told him that he should make the decision for me and I would go with it.

Less than five minutes after that conversation, my branch manager summoned me into his office. He also wanted to know my decision. Would I stay with him or did I prefer the other manager? I already knew that there was no love lost between both men and I didn't want to be cannon fodder in their office battle. I repeated the same thing I had said to the other. He wanted me to send a mail stating my preference but I respectfully declined, maintaining that he should make the choice for me instead.

A few minutes later, my branch manager replied the initial mail, stating that I preferred to stay with him. As if on cue, HR acknowledged the decision almost immediately. Of course, the other manager was furious and called me right away but I explained to him that as he could see, no mail emanated from me. The matter was therefore laid to rest.

Be tactful, especially when you're relating with several superiors. It's important to know how to say the right things at work. You should not lie but you carefully choose what you say, without leading to offense. According to the Oxford dictionary, tact is 'the skill and sensitivity in dealing with others or with difficult issues'. It's a critical factor in emotional intelligence.

Another area where tact is required is when responding to queries. Sometimes, you may get one in the line of duty, especially where there has been an infraction or a breach of company rules or policies. But answering a query requires diplomacy. Never respond when you're angry and don't be rash. Take some time to cool off. Consider the circumstances surrounding the event that led to the query and be as dispassionate as possible. State the facts as clearly and be as inoffensive as possible.

If you're culpable then take responsibility and be sincerely apologetic. Let remorse be evident in your response. Never try to shift the blame on others if the facts are to the contrary. Even when you know that you did not deserve the query, still follow the same pattern. Don't try to justify anything. Don't take anything personal.

Your response usually communicate your attitude so be careful in your expression. Choose your words carefully to avoid being misinterpreted. If it's a major issue, then you can also ask a colleague for advice or have them go through your intended response. Remember however that the entire responsibility for whatever you send remains yours.

Indeed, any staff who applies tact in his dealings will be in the good books of his supervisors and colleagues.

10

LESSON TEN

GET A MENTOR*

> *"Mentoring is a brain to pick, an ear to listen and a push in the right direction"*
> **- John C. Crosby**

A few years ago, I was in South Africa and I stayed at my mentor's house while he was back in Nigeria. During my stay, he called and gave me directions to a particular location that I had to access by taking the Gautrain. He was on the phone with me almost throughout the journey, which took about 2 hours. Eventually, I arrived at a choice piece of real estate. I have not read in any book what he taught me about real estate that night.

One evening after that period, he called and asked me to drive towards a place called Siun along Sagamu-Abeokuta road. I met him there and he taught me about positioning for opportunities with the benefit of foresight.

As I left my car to ride with him, he took me around that environment. That was when he opened my eyes to the transformation happening in that area and how that axis will open up within 10 years. He taught me about taking risks.

I have also learnt about charity through him. I have observed how he works extremely hard even for his age. I have seen how content he is and learnt that one of his greatest strengths is his humility. Through him I have learnt that you can have gold and still be godly. I have observed his tremendous love for his wife, even in the midst of challenges.

Even though he is absolutely well to do (putting it mildly), I have never even asked him to patronize any of the 7 banks that I have worked for. The few times that he did, the request came from him personally. On one occasion, he expressed his surprise that I had never discussed the issue of account opening with him. I have never asked him for special favours, not even for any connection. All I want is his wisdom. For me, in accordance with Proverbs 4:7, wisdom is the principal thing, not money and definitely, not connections.

I have benefitted immensely from my mentor's wealth of knowledge, not from his deep pockets. And this is where so many people miss it now. I've been contacted by a number of people for mentorship but I ended up finding out that what they needed was either a meal ticket or some form of favour.

It breaks my heart when I see people make serious errors in judgment by choosing what is inconsequential to their lives. There was an instance when I refused a young man some financial favour and he decided to cut ties with me. Till date, every text I send goes unanswered. Meanwhile, he was the one who requested for personal mentoring!

There are things I say to those who want me to mentor them. I trust that these tips can also guide you to maximize such relationships:

1. A mentor is not a meal ticket. I don't provide money; I provide wisdom. Many people don't need mentors. What they need are business partners. Don't ask your mentor for financial favours. at will ruin the relationship. Rather ask for wisdom and guidance. If you get the wisdom then money is just a matter of time.

2. A mentor cannot solve all problems. I don't have a magic wand. I can talk to you about finance, leadership, purpose, business, and excellence but I can't tell you whom to marry, for instance. I'm not the Holy Spirit. I don't know all things.

Certain things still remain your responsibility, including the decisions that you make. Your decisions are ultimately yours. Remember that even if I counsel you, your failures are strictly yours. I can't take responsibility on your behalf. Recognize the expertise of your mentor.

3. Mentoring is a long term relationship. It is not short term. I have known my mentor for about 17 years and our relationship is still going strong. Be ready to go the whole hog with me. You can't get all you need in one month or even one year. The best things in life unfold gradually.

4. Mentoring requires patience. You may want something badly but you must be patient enough to get it. I'm going to try your patience- sometimes deliberately to know if you really want it that bad. I won't pick your calls sometimes. I won't respond to your mails at other times. All I'm trying to do is to stoke up the hunger within you. The hungrier you are, the easier it is to pass across timeless wisdom.

5. Mentees must curry the favour of the mentor. I have what you want and you must devise all means possible to get it from me. Stop visiting your mentors empty handed. I am not begging for a gift from you but if you want to collect something from me, you must release what is in your hands. Prov. 18:16 (Message Translation) says that a gift gets attention; it buys the attention of eminent people.

6. A mentor is not going to find you. Rather, you should find the mentor. I believe this is clear enough.

7. The greatest resource a mentor can give to the mentee is time. Use this time wisely. Ask questions. Observe quietly. Don't waste that time. Value it. Appreciate it. The greatest commodity that I have is not money. It's my time.

8. A mentor is not your friend. Don't take that relationship for granted. I do not take my mentor for granted. I know his house but I don't barge in on him. I have access to him but I don't abuse that access. I don't call him at odd hours. I don't get too familiar.

So, dear mentee, a mentor helps you to prepare for the future. In the words of Isaac Newton, "If I have seen further than others, it is by standing on the shoulders of giants." A mentor provides ideas, thoughts and insights that elevate your thinking. A mentor can push you to the next level. A mentor nurtures. A mentor shares valuable life lessons. A mentor shares their experiences with you so that you don't have to repeat their mistakes.

Get a mentor for your career.

I trust this guide helps you.

This was an article I wrote and originally titled "Dear Young Man: A Guide To Mentoring" on July 17, 2017. It went viral on social media.

11

LESSON ELEVEN

CHANGE JOBS THE SMART WAY

> *"I am not a product of my circumstances. I am a product of my decisions"*
> **- Stephen Covey**

I learnt quite early in my career that one could either move vertically or horizontally. Vertical movement in this context being within the same organization and involves you waiting for a promotion cycle while horizontal movements are outside the organization to other companies, within or outside the same sector.

From the onset, you need to de ne how you intend to maximize your career. Some people are interested in a career where they can settle down and grow with the organization. Due to certain peculiarities or situations such as taking up an additional degree or qualification, a new marriage or building a home, they may also find vertical movements steady and appealing. The truth is that your focus is determined by your aspirations.

Then there are those, like me, whose paths require a lot of horizontal movement in order to achieve their goals. However, every horizontal movement comes with its own risks. It is much easier and more convenient to stay in a company where you are familiar with the people, system and culture aspiring to vertical movement. For every horizontal movement, there is some learning and unlearning to be done

When I started my banking career at age 25, I set a goal to be a general manager at 40. So I developed a 15-year plan. I figured that staying with a single company and expecting to be promoted on an average of every 3 years (if I'm lucky and become a high-flier) wouldn't cut it because the best I would have been promoted is a maximum of 5 times. I knew that, depending on the organization, it would take about 12 steps to get to my goal in the planned time frame. My plan was therefore to concentrate on horizontal movements, while taking advantage of vertical movements as the opportunities presented themselves.

Changing jobs can be tricky. There are some fundamental questions that you need to answer: Why are you changing jobs? What's your prime motivation? How will the new job help you in meeting your personal goals?

Even though money does matter, I counsel people not to change jobs only for bigger pay. That should not be your single consideration. I've realized that the euphoria of increased salary lasts for only a few months as expenses always rise to meet income. This is why you should consider other benefits and allowances that come with the job.

Find out about their health insurance package. I once worked for an organization which had a good family health plan. Therefore, when my wife delivered our daughter via caesarean section, the bill was covered in full. I believe that it is one of the reasons that more females have worked almost their entire lives in that company than males. In that same organization taking your leave was sacrosanct and people were actively encouraged to go on vacation.

Consider the work environment. You may need to speak to someone you know in the prospective company. Will you be able to thrive under such work environment? Do they have the products and services that will assist you in delivering on the commitments you gave during the interview process? If they don't, then you may not be able to migrate your existing relationships successfully (especially as a sales person).

What's the brand like? Is there brand acceptance and a positive perception? What kind of structure do they operate? Don't jump into a company where you need to start explaining the wisdom in your move to others. If you have to, ensure that it comes at a premium. This will compensate for any inconvenience you will face.

What is the organizational culture like? Does it allow for innovation and creativity? Will it allow you to thrive? Is it an environment that kills innovations and rewards mediocrity? How often do they evolve? Who are the Management team? Any international affiliates? Don't forget we are on the global stage now and preparation for global competitiveness is extremely imperative now for relevance in dealing with today's opportunities.

Will your move challenge your potential? Are there opportunities for growth? These are factors to critically consider. It was until I moved to a particular organization that I discovered that some staff had been on probation for two years and they were not poor performers! I also encountered people who had been on the same grade for many years. Some of them had stagnated for up to 6 years. Yet the company was one of the highest paying at that time. This was why many were disgruntled. Staff tiptoed around the office and it was a generally toxic environment. I stayed there only for 8 months.

Will the organization help you meet your personal goals? I once worked in a company where the training and personal development opportunities mattered to me most. I often went on training programmes almost on a monthly basis. At another organization, I had the opportunity of being on the training faculty whenever new hires went through their induction. That was truly important to me. I would even have paid for the opportunity, if I had to.

Look at your career and build a good trajectory while changing jobs. Negotiate well during interviews to ensure you get a good deal. Starting over at a new job requires imbibing a new culture and the learning curve may be short. It is also usual to go through a period of probation.

If you are an experienced hire then the expectation may be high, particularly in a performance-driven environment. Also, if you move in the middle of an organizational restructuring, such as a merger or acquisition, and staff rationalization is involved, then you could be caught up in the kerfuffle. This is when Last In First Out (LIFO) may be applied. You must be mentally prepared for all these in order to maximize your move.

Remember to maximize your network. Be friendly with other people in your industry. I've gotten new offers through colleagues who told me about vacancies at their own companies. Keep your ears to the ground. Ensure that you're on professional social networking sites such as LinkedIn.

Be a very industrious staff and be loyal to your boss. The fact is that if your boss moves and needs to form a new team, they would most likely call for those they know. Remember that a value adding staff will never lack the opportunity to show that they can add value.

12

LESSON TWELVE

BE FRIENDLY

> "Lead a life that will make you kindly and friendly to everyone about you and you will be surprised what a happy life you will lead"
> - *Charles M. Schwab*

If you will go far in your career, you must cultivate and nurture relationships. We all pray for God's blessings and the truth is that He sends them through human beings. I got my first banking job through a friend who came all the way from Bayelsa state to Port Harcourt to show me a newspaper cutting of the job advertisement. I worked at that particular job for two years.

The next job came about one evening as I drove into my house after work. My neighbour who was a senior banker beckoned to me. He had also just parked his car. He asked if I was interested in working with a new bank that had just come to town. By then, I had learnt never to say no to opportunities. So he told me to see a certain colleague of his at his workplace the following day. I did and realized that this person had been recruited as the branch manager of the new bank and he was looking for staff. To cut a long story short, I got hired.

I was at the job for eight months when I got a call from a woman that I had never met before. She introduced herself and said that someone had recommended me as a good salesperson and she was looking for staff for her branch. I later discovered that her cousin attended the same church with me and he was the one who gave her my contact details. She hired me.

A few years later, the banking consolidation of the Charles Soludo era at the Central Bank of Nigeria caught up with banks. There was so much uncertainty and strong rumours of downsizing everywhere. I was a team lead then and one of those days, I was discussing with the lead of our second team when he mentioned that he could actually give me a referral to his previous bank. He then gave me a note on his business card to his former branch manager. I took the note to that branch manager who immediately set up an interview panel for me and that was how I got my next job.

I came to work on a particular Saturday a couple of years down the line and was in conversation with a senior colleague. I had worked with this particular person in two different banks before and he had been my branch manager in the last. However, we worked out of different branches at this point.

I asked him about a particular staff whose absence I noticed. That was when he told me that the fellow had joined a new bank in town. I expressed surprise as I didn't know that the bank had made a foray into Ibadan. He then said that the bank's recruiting officer for the branch was his friend and asked me if I was interested. As usual, I replied in the affirmative. I met the person that same day and got to take my test and interviews the following week. I was hired.

After about five years in this particular bank, during which I had changed branches and locations, my former line manager called me to join her. She had moved to another bank and wanted me to work with her. I was interviewed and hired. This same lady got another role in yet another bank and requested that I join her again. I was interviewed and hired yet again.

Be friendly at work. Bond well with your colleagues. Don't operate in your own silo. Network with friends, explore to know people in your sphere of interest. Spend some time after work to share some common interests. Attend social gatherings with them. Participate freely in various activities and chat groups that you belong to. People will freely share opportunities with you once they are comfortable with you.

Don't be difficult to work with. Be willing to help out. Let people find you reliable and trustworthy. Loyalty to your superior is non-negotiable. Watch their backs and they will watch yours also.

I indeed have had many opportunities come my way, but they were mostly through friendships and positive work experiences with colleagues who felt comfortable enough to recommend me. This is what I refer to as *relational intelligence*.

13

LESSON THIRTEEN

DON'T BURN BRIDGES

> *"Don't burn bridges. You'll be surprised how many times you have to cross the same river"*
> *- H. Jackson Brown, Jr.*

In the course of your career, you will go through different kinds of experiences. You will meet with and work with different people. You will be faced with circumstances and situations that will challenge you. In spite of all these things, never burn bridges.

How you leave an organization matters. You must exit properly, regardless of the circumstances surrounding your move. In one of the places that I once worked a staff left impolitely, against all advice given to her. She was arrogant and obnoxious about it and it was too glaring that she had issues with her boss.

About a month later, a staff in another branch called me. He wanted my opinion on this same lady. Apparently, she wanted to return to the bank via his branch. I informed him about what had transpired and of course, that was the end of her job interview. When you exit a door, shut it carefully as you may later need it on an unexpected return journey.

When you are at an interview, never speak ill of your bosses or subordinates. Once a candidate I am interviewing does that, it is a 'No' from me as I believe that they would certainly do the same to me later. Never badmouth your former company or organization. There are no perfect companies. While working in your team, be free to disagree with your colleagues without being disagreeable. Be quick to resolve issues and never take any work disagreements personal.

Over the course of my career, I have had very cordial relationships with all my supervisors. In fact, some of them have filled reference forms on my behalf to other organizations. I recall the time a top-level executive joined our company and became my supervisor. It was just when I had gone through some bitter and humiliating experience at work. Coincidentally, I got an offer from another bank and I made up my mind to leave.

It was around this period that he came on a working visit to some of my customers who were upcountry. I hosted him and was even at his hotel till late in the night. It was during a period of fuel scarcity and I had to seriously look for fuel for his return trip to the head office.

All the while, I had my offer letter in my pocket and I could have just walked away. But since I try never to burn bridges, I worked hard not to make it obvious I was leaving. I also felt that it was improper to discuss my resignation with my supervisor during his visit I therefore waited for him to return to Lagos and a few hours after, I also travelled to see him. One way or the other, I got to his office before he did and waited. When he arrived, he was of course, shocked to see me.

He took off his jacket in astonishment when I told him why I had come. I showed him my new offer. He appreciated the way I handled the matter, as he was fully aware of the humbling circumstances that I had been through at work. He told me that if I realised that I didn't like my new employment, I should call him and he would be ready to take me back. I thanked him profusely and he prayed for me.

A few months later, I needed a letter of reference from him. His personal assistant called me and said that I should send in a draft, which I did. When he sent the reference back on his letter-head, it was exactly what I had drafted. He didn't change anything, not a word or sentence. All he did was to append his signature!

Prepare your exit honourably. Consider your role or job to have been a privilege as there are several hundreds who could have done it better. Be humble in your approach and be grateful for the opportunity as you discuss your exit with your supervisor or line manager. The rule of thumb is to always discuss before dropping your letter of resignation. A face-to-face discussion is usually better. Make the discussion personal.

Go through all exit protocols as required by your current employer. If there are forms to be filled, fill them. Your resignation must be simple and full of appreciation to the boss and organization. Don't express any bile or angst, even if you have any. Remember that whatever is written down goes on record. I also consider that tendering a resignation via email is rude and condescending.

Life can be funny. You may end up needing a reference from your former boss. Or sometime down the line, you may even meet the same person in another organization. Never burn bridges.

14

LESSON FOURTEEN

NEVER CHASE MONEY

> *"Chase the vision, not the money; the money will end up following you"*
> **- Tony Hsieh**

I was over the moon when I got the employment offer. The new salary was a fifty per cent increase over what I earned at the time and I had started thinking of how I could put the extra money to good use. I could do with a change of vehicle. It was time for my status to change. I was so happy to show my wife the new offer, but I noticed that she didn't particularly share my enthusiasm.

Later that night, she woke me up from sleep. I sat up, knowing that there was a serious issue at hand. She asked whether I'd given much thought to the job offer. I replied in the affirmative. Next, she asked if I was ready to move to Ogbomoso. I gave another yes.

It made sense to me because at that time, I was working in Ibadan, the state capital, as a relationship manager but I was going to be a branch manager in Ogbomoso, which was a different town. In addition, I would get an official car, something I didn't have in Ibadan.

Finally, she asked me some questions that I couldn't answer: how would I want my resume to read in five years? Would I be able to satisfactorily explain why I left a city like Ibadan for a place considered behind in terms of development, economy, size and potentials? And would it be easy to make a transition from Ogbomoso to Lagos, for instance?

She counselled me not to be carried away by the official car and the extra disposable income. She then threw in a clincher: Do I want to chase my career or chase money? that discussion put everything into proper perspective for me. If I chase money, then money will continue to be elusive but if I chase my career, money will eventually come.

Many people make that mistake. they are easily swayed by the promise of a better salary, even when there will be no obvious career progression. At the inception of your career, money must never be your only motivation. You must choose career advancement over cash. I have since then counselled a lot of people who were in my shoes not to make such mistakes. People who do so are not likely to last long.

Back to my story, I didn't take the offer. Incidentally the bank went down a few years after, so I may have been rendered jobless. And of course, I made an easy transition to Lagos from Ibadan eventually which opened countless opportunities.

15

LESSON FIFTEEN

FIND PROBLEMS AND SOLVE THEM

> "Running away om a problem only increases the distance om the solution"
> - *Anonymous*

In 2009, I was dissatisfied with my career and I decided that I needed to take on a new challenge. I felt that my career had plateaued. Even though I had worked for 4 different banks by then, I had remained in one town (Ibadan) from the inception of my career. I just knew that there could be more. Fortunately, an internal advertisement for a role in Lagos came up and I was very willing to try. I applied and was interviewed.

Thereafter, I was informed that the role was no longer available. I was offered another one with a caveat—it was a very tough branch that had not been profitable in about five years! Now, in the banking sector, profitability is the bottom line. I was also told that the last three branch managers had lost their jobs because they could not solve the problem. Furthermore, the staff at that location had the worst appraisal scores and they were always bottom of the pack. Obviously, the stories I heard were very discouraging. Yet I told my interviewer that I was ready to take the job.

A few days after our discussion, she called to check. I still insisted on taking the role. She expressed her reservations that I had never worked in Lagos before but I told her that irrespective of location, clients have the same needs and wants. She then told me that she would also keep my current role in Ibadan open for three months should I change my mind. I recall retorting that anyone that puts his hand on the plough and looks back is unfit for the kingdom of heaven. We both laughed at my scriptural inference, but I meant it.

I assumed the role and got to work immediately. The situation was dismal indeed. The figures were bad. Customer service was poor, and I met very disoriented and unenthusiastic staff. I was however undaunted.

I went through the books and made my strategy to improve sales. I worked on staff morale and held daily meetings to review our activities. I started a weekly motivational mail list. I encouraged cold calls and led by example. I celebrated each win, irrespective of the ticket size. I asked the back office and support staff to also contribute to sales by starting from family and friends and later on, referrals. I asked staff to start taking personal responsibility for our situation.

By the fourth month, the branch made profit for the first time in five years. We went further to increase our profit so rapidly that the whole bank took note. By the end of that year, our appraisals turned out to be some of the best in the bank. The following year, I was transferred to head the biggest branch in the bank and I got a promotion in a short while.

If I had remained in Ibadan, which had become my comfort zone, I would have become anonymous and possibly stayed on the same grade for a long time.

Many people run away from problems and challenges but if you want to move up rapidly in your career then you must look for problems to solve. The more problems you solve, the higher you go. The lessons you learn from challenges help you to develop and utilize skills that have never been used and sharpen your ability to validate certain decisions about problem solving.

Never be scared of making mistakes as you're ten times better than someone who has never tried. At the very least, it helps you keep a knowledge base of 'how not to fail'. I usually tell people that promotion is not a right. No one promotes you for how long you have stayed at a role or for how long you have worked for an institution. Promotion is earned and the way to earn it is by providing answers to problems.

A final word: pay by hour is the lowest level of pay. The highest is to be paid according to the problems that you solve.

LESSON SIXTEEN

THE BEST ADVICE I RECEIVED IN MY CAREER

> "Light Shines Brightest In Darkness"

It was late 2011. I'd worked for the same international financial institution across Ibadan and Lagos and was managing my third branch in 5 years. That particular year, I had an excellent appraisal. I also received an award for the largest volume of a particular deal in Africa. The company sent me and some colleagues on an all-expenses-paid trip to Dubai as a reward for exceeding our targets on certain products. I had the visibility and prominence in that company. I was managing the largest branch of that organization in Nigeria and my career was at an all-time high.

Suddenly, I got an offer to work with another organization. This new company was going through a very trying time. It had mutated over the years and had just been nationalized (taken over by the regulatory authorities) with a newly appointed management. Honestly, they really did not have an exciting history.

But the offer was good. It came with a promotion, a good salary, and the other benefits were attractive. I was going to be migrating from middle management to senior management. So, I was torn. Would I leave a world-class organization where I was recognized as a top performer for a challenged and nationalized organization with a not too enviable past? That would mean leaving certainty for uncertainty.

Was I willing to take the plunge? The more I reflected on the offer, the more unattractive it seemed. For me, everything is not about money. It was one of the toughest decisions I've ever had to make in my career.

I told a few close clients about the offer and they didn't mince words in telling me that I would be making a mistake if I accepted it. One particular customer, who was fond of me and was an older brother of one of my bosses, was unequivocally against my move. He even sent me a text message to further dissuade me. I was really confused and on the verge of turning down the offer.

Then I travelled to Ibadan for an event. There, I met a friend I'd not seen or heard from in years. We chitchatted for a while and the discussion veered to our careers. I told him where I was and mentioned in passing the new offer that I had just gotten.

He looked straight at me and asked if there was anything that I could achieve in the current organization that had never been done before. I thought very hard. The organization is in several countries around the world with thousands of employees. No matter what I did therefore, I would always be a small fish in a big bowl. He then said that on the contrary, every little achievement of mine in the new place would be significant. Little steps would look big and I could easily become a hero.

My friend then went on to make a statement that I've not forgotten since that hot afternoon in 2011.

He said, "Light shines brightest in darkness. I advise you take the offer".

Immediately he said that, it felt like a veil was lifted from my mind. The confusion was gone, and I knew precisely that taking the offer was what I was meant to do under the circumstances. It would afford me to be that big fish in a small bowl. I took the offer and it was one of the best things that happened to me.

I had a wonderful time there. At a point, I managed two regions at the same time. I sat on various committees at the instance of the managing director and later received a letter of commendation for my performance. I was also made part of the training faculty for the organization. I have never regretted the move. It was a very risky one, but it definitely paid off.

17

LESSON SEVENTEEN

BE SPONTANEOUS. BE FLUID*

> "Find a way to say yes to things. Say yes to invitations to a new country, say yes to meet new friends, say yes to learn something new. Yes is how you get your first job and your next job and your spouse and even your kids"
>
> **- Eric Schmidt**

As you build your career, two major ingredients are necessary for your development: spontaneity and fluidity. After I finished my national youth service, I got a job as a salesman in a company that was a major distributor for a leading manufacturer of fast-moving consumer goods in Nigeria.

I was just about concluding my documentation towards resumption when the human resources staff asked if I could drive. Without thinking, I gave a positive answer immediately. The truth however was that I couldn't drive very well at the time. He threw the keys at me without further enquiry, so I walked confidently to the bus and started it. I had a female sales partner who worked with me then. Unfortunately, I gave her some real trouble with my driving! But that was a demonstration of spontaneity.

Spontaneity is the ability for you to think on your feet and take advantage of any occasion almost on reflex. Many opportunities will arise and you need to avail yourself of them right away. You usually won't have a lot of time to think and the decision would need to be taken on the spur of the moment. It also has to be the right one.

Fluidity was at play when I decided to relocate from Ibadan, a very relaxed and easy-going city to an energy-sapping and rigorous place like Lagos. I had no previous experience of working in Lagos. Even worse, I had to put up with a friend for six months until I could afford to rent a place for myself.

It is the property of a fluid to take on the shape of any container that it occupies. Fluidity is thus the ability to adapt to any situation, no matter the circumstance. This is a major characteristic that anyone interested in pursuing a career must have. You should be ready to work anywhere, in any role, and with anyone.

As anticipated, my fluidity paid off. I got bigger opportunities in Lagos which I couldn't have gotten had I stayed in Ibadan. After just a year, I got transferred to the biggest branch of that bank in West Africa as the branch manager!

Spontaneity helps you to quickly seize the moment while fluidity ensures that you are able to move from one career, skill, location, or focus to another.

*I owe the title of this chapter to Olusola Amusan of Microsoft who was present at a career event where I shared the incidents described here. He summarized them as spontaneity and fluidity.

18

LESSON EIGHTEEN

DON'T BE A ONE-ROLE SPECIALIST

> *"Be willing to change because life won't stay the same"*
> *-Anonymous*

One of the greatest career mistakes you can ever make is to confine yourself to one function. In an ever-changing and dynamic work environment, you must be ready to switch from one role to another within the demands of your organization. Even if you work in a professional firm or an organization that has only one focus, you should still explore other ways of doing things. You need to be flexible and open to change.

I started my career in the operations unit of a bank and was tutored in the rudiments of banking operations and I worked across various areas within the department. However, I was ready to move to sales the moment I got the opportunity. Meanwhile, many of my colleagues did not want to take on any sales role because of the challenges and high mortality rates.

I decided to broaden the scope of my career and not limit myself. Not even the fear of being right-sized because of the inability to meet sales target was enough to deter me. That step I took has certainly paid off as the flexibility helped my career in no small measure.

Over the years, I've witnessed people who could only function in a specific role and couldn't cope once any realignment or reshuffling happened. If you will be outstanding in your career then you should be prepared for change because the only thing constant is change. therefore, nothing should catch you unawares.

You may be in the back office today but you should be well informed about what the people in sales or the front office do. Have transferable skills and also increase your skillset while on your current role. You can do this by way of continuous personal development and training. Go for courses, even in areas where you are not familiar with. It is good for your resume, as you will have a wide range of experience.

One-role specialists are limited in their scope and reach. Eventually, they become stuck in their ways and do not easily adapt to the changing demands of their organization and career. Jobs are changing: same reason you should evolve, be open minded, be receptive of knowledge, volunteer to learn new things and engage new technology as this enhances your ability to transit into a new career if need be.

One-role specialists are the first casualties during periods of business recession or economic decline. Don't limit yourself by restricting yourself to certain roles.

LESSON NINETEEN

COMMUNICATION SKILLS ARE IMPORTANT

> *"Communication is your ticket to success, if you pay attention and learn to do it effectively"*
> **-Theo Gold**

I got a mail to attend a competency assessment session at one of the foremost consulting firms in Nigeria. It was for all the senior management staff at my organization. No one had a clue of what the format would be.

I was the first person to interface with the consulting firm. As I arrived at their office in highbrow Victoria Island, Lagos, I still did not know what to expect. A lady led me into a small room where I sat down for a while before she ushered me into a much larger room. There stood a man positioned with a video camera.

The lady then handed me a printed sheet of paper containing eight scenarios. The instruction was to choose one of them for my presentation. I had just 30 minutes for that part of the interview. I ran through the list. There was none that I couldn't have answered.

One however caught my attention: "You became the MD of the bank a few months ago and the bank has been given an award, which you have to receive on behalf of the bank. You are to write your acceptance speech and present it to the audience". I sat down to work and scribbled a few thoughts on paper. After a few minutes, I was ready to make a presentation.

I looked directly at the camera and gave my speech. I punctuated where necessary, paused for effect, pronounced my words well, and gesticulated to reduce the monotony. There was no reason to cut the tape as I finished the recording in one fell swoop. The lady smiled and informed me that I could do it up to three times if I wanted to but I told her it wasn't necessary.

Of course, I knew that they were checking up on our communication and presentation skills. It would have been simply too late for anyone to start learning these at this point.

According to Tony Wagner, the seven critical survival skills for the future are: critical thinking and problem solving, collaboration, agility and adaptability, initiative and entrepreneurship, oral and written communication, assessing and analysing information, and curiosity and imagination. I believe, however, that the most critical out of the seven skills is communication.

You can never rise beyond the level of your communication. The more effective you are as a communicator, the more effective you become and the greater your prospects of climbing up the ladder. This is why you must spend time to develop your communication skills—oral and written.

You must learn how to write well: from sending emails to writing official letters and internal memos. If you work in a large organization, there is every possibility that you may not know all the staff. Thus, most people will judge you and relate to you based on the quality of communication that you have displayed, especially the first time. Impressions are created by how you write or speak.

Reading books will help to expand your vocabulary and also develop both oral and written communication. So, read newspapers and journals. I follow certain newspaper columnists who write extremely well. Read specialized journals meant for your sector. You should also have a dictionary handy so that you can always look up the meaning of words and their appropriate use.

Always use your spell checker when sending out emails or letters. Don't be in a hurry to click send. Review carefully because once you send it, you may not be able to recall the message. Write in long hand and avoid abbreviations. Most individuals I come across now use abbreviations just as if they are sending personal text messages on their phones. This habit has even crept into writing official correspondence. Go for courses on business communication, if you must.

Closely linked to communication is the art of presentation. As you climb up the ladder, you will start engaging more people and may be required to make presentations to individuals or groups. Your ability to navigate through the presentations while capturing the attention of your audience within the time given is a skill that must be developed. This often comes with practice and the more you practice, the better you become.

This is why I usually hold monthly management profitability report sessions (popularly called MPR in the banking sector) where all my team members come to present their scorecard and plans for the new month. Each person comes with their slides and they make presentations to the audience. In the process, their communication and presentation skills are developed and further polished.

On Saturday, June 23, 2018, I received a call that the Vice President of Nigeria would be in Ibadan for a town hall session the following Tuesday and I was requested to give a speech to the youth in attendance. This was incredible news to me. So the day came and the event took off with me as a co-panelist during the first session.

Later on, the Vice President arrived and the programme had to be rearranged because of his schedule. One of his aides beckoned and asked if I could sum up my speech in 15 minutes. Of course, I answered. He beckoned again later and asked if I could do it in 5 minutes. I answered affirmatively. After the national anthem, I was called up for my speech. The VP and the Governor of Oyo State were seated, among other dignitaries.

As I walked up the stage, I muttered a prayer. I remembered the words of Abraham Lincoln, "I will prepare myself and one day my chance will come". I looked at several cameras that clicked away. I was the cynosure of all eyes. It was a moment that may end up defining me.

Yet again, the VP's aide stepped up to me and whispered into my ears, "Please can you do this in 2 minutes?" I nodded. Even one minute was okay for me. After all, opportunities like these don't come every time. I took the microphone, saluted the VP and the Governor and charged the audience. I made my presentation within the allotted time given. It was short, but it was sharp and punchy. I walked off the stage to a thunderous applause.

Your ability to communicate effectively and make outstanding presentations will differentiate you from your peers.

20

LESSON TWENTY

DON'T DO IT IF YOU CAN'T TALK ABOUT IT

> "With integrity, you have nothing to fear, since you have nothing to hide"
> **- Zig Ziglar**

I put a random call through to my former boss after a long time of not being in touch. He was my branch manager many years before, when I was a relationship manager, but I had since moved to another organization. I mentioned in passing that I was looking at recruiting one of
the guys who worked with us earlier.

His next statement stopped me in my tracks and I've never forgotten till this day. His exact words, "Don't try it. That guy is not a banker; he's a bandit". He then reeled out several dubious acts that were uncovered about the fellow and how he was let off ignominiously. I had no idea until then. Immediately, I dropped all plans of hiring him.

Integrity is the most important characteristic in the work place for me. It is non-negotiable. Without it your career would be easily truncated. A seeming lack of discretion can destroy a career that you have built for years.

Not even competence can take the place of integrity because a person can be trained but lack of integrity is a character flaw. This is why I'd rather hire someone who has integrity but is not as competent, than take someone who is highly competent but lacks integrity.

Many years ago, there was a high incidence of round tripping going on in the industry because of the foreign exchange situation in Nigeria. So one day I called a staff meeting and warned everyone not to get involved. I recall that I threatened to personally escalate anyone found wanting.

After the meeting, one of my staff came to my office. He looked very sober. He told me that he was very touched as I spoke during the meeting and it was as if I was talking to him directly. He then brought out about 10 international passports from his inner jacket.

He explained how he wanted to use those passports to obtain foreign exchange dubiously and then sell in the parallel market for gain. He went on to promise that based on my admonition, he wasn't going to proceed with his plans. I counselled him and spoke to him about maintaining integrity. About a year later, however, he got involved in another terrible incident and was fired for his dishonesty.

In 2013, I processed a loan facility for a customer and it was approved. The customer was excited. He had almost lost hope because some other financial institutions had already declined his request. He later invited me to his house at an upscale location in Ikoyi, Lagos. I decided to visit him with his account officer as by practice, I hardly visit customers alone.

From the customer's countenance, I could tell that he was expecting to see only me. After exchanging pleasantries, he invited me to his library while the account officer was in the living room. He thanked me profusely for assisting him but wanted to find out how much I would like to collect as my share from the approved loan. I told him in plain terms that I don't engage in such acts. He was shocked when I only told him to ensure that he utilized the funds well and return same in good time as stated in the offer.

Along the line, I had to come hard on him when he defaulted on the facility but I wouldn't have had that boldness if I had compromised. He told everyone around how much he respected me based on our encounter. Till today, I maintain a very cordial and strong relationship with this customer and he has now become a personal friend. At the risk of sounding immodest, I can openly say that I've never received gratification from any customer for granting a loan or just doing my job.

You need to walk in line with the ground rules in your organization. Most establishments have their guidelines on accepting gifts from customers. Don't flout such policies. At one organization that I worked, there was a gift register where any gift above a certain monetary value was to be declared and the gift submitted.

Where such rules are not in place, work ethics demand that any gift that could compromise your judgment should not be taken. Whatever you cannot freely disclose to everyone should never be indulged in. If you can't talk about it, then don't do it. I will rather be tired for poor performance than be fired for a lack of integrity.

And don't put yourself in a situation where you can be compromised. I usually encourage my team to go out in pairs. It's easier to work on a lone staff than two who are a part of a team. Never expect favours from a client. If you don't expect favours, you won't be disappointed. You should also endeavour to live below your means. When you do, you won't be under any pressure to keep up appearances.

Integrity however goes beyond the issue of receiving gratification at work. It includes selling the right products to customers and being honest in our dealings with them. Integrity involves owning up and taking personal responsibility when mistakes are made, irrespective of the consequences. We also need to reinforce integrity by rewarding acts of honesty.

Be honest in all your dealings. Honesty is still the best policy and will never go out of fashion. Be absolutely transparent. Watch those you associate with. Be a stickler for rules. Once you're known for this quality of character, most shady colleagues will avoid you. Build your career with peace of mind. Those who play on the fast lane usually don't last in play.

LESSON TWENTY ONE

COMPETENCE IS KEY

"If you think you can do it, that's confidence. If you do it, that's competence"
- Morris Code

At one point in your career, you will get to lead a team. Three major ingredients are necessary for building and leading a great team.

They are character, competence and communication. I've already dealt with the issue of communication and character (integrity).

Any career that would be long and fulfilling needs to have competence at its core. Competence is a combination of ability and knowledge. It simply means that you know what to do and are able to do it. It involves the what to do and how to do it.

You must understand the intricacies of your job role in order to be outstanding. You must also demonstrate a high level of proficiency at carrying out that role. Aspire to be the go-to person in specific areas of your job. This means that you're several steps ahead of your contemporaries.

When you're perceived as competent, your colleagues look up to you and your superiors look for you. The keyword here is perception, because at a certain stage in your career it's no longer about what you have done but what you are perceived to be able to do. Competence improves or increases that perception.

It involves hard work. Demonstrating that you're good at what you do is not a tea party. You must have a thorough understanding of the job as well as the issues, and the challenges. Then you need to combine your knowledge with skills and good judgment

Competence is demonstrated both in theory and practice. When I started my banking career, I spent hours reading up on several areas, most especially on credit analysis. I asked questions from my superiors. I did not relent because I wanted to be the best. I made up my mind that there was no question any client could ask that I wouldn't be able to answer immediately.

At that period, I had a supervisor who was interested in my career growth and pushed me to the limit. I was a few days on the sales role when he made me write my first credit memorandum. I went through all the previous credit files and didn't leave the office that night until 11pm. In addition, I discovered that the more I actually did the work the more I became proficient at it.

Your competence in any area is tested when there are problems to solve. I got a bigger role in a particular organization because I was able to execute a clear strategy that turned around a branch which had made consistent losses for 5 years. If you start working on your capacity when you're faced with a challenge, then you're too late. You should project into your future and start working on the required skills for tomorrow, today.

So, you need to learn. Acquire knowledge in an area more than others. Go deeper. Read. Know everything there is to know about your specific field. Then go beyond this to applying that knowledge to the situation. Be creative about it. Find a way to do it better and immediately start teaching others. The more you teach others, the better you become.

LESSON TWENTY TWO

REGULARLY SET AND UPDATE YOUR GOALS

> *"If you don't design your own life plan, chances are that you'll fall into someone else's plan. And guess what they have planned for you? Not much"*
>
> ***-Jim Rohn***

In 2007, I brought out a notebook and decided to revisit my already audacious career goals. I still wanted to become a general manager by age 40. At the time, I was just an assistant manager and already 32 years old, meaning that I only had 8 years to achieve it. I knew that I had to be very aggressive and make more ambitious moves, not waiting for the annual promotion cycles.

I went on to outline the steps that were left: deputy manager, manager, senior manager, assistant general manager, deputy general manager, and then general manager. I would need to transit those 6 levels within 8 years.

Therefore, I worked on myself, because if I wanted to move faster, I had to display a great capacity. The better my skills and competence, the easier it would be to assume responsibility for new levels. I also knew that my location at that time (Ibadan) would limit my ability to rise up the ladder as there were few opportunities for career progression there. I would not have a chance in the world of meeting my goal if I did not find my way to Lagos, the commercial centre of Nigeria.

So I took calculated risks. I attended interviews, made bold commitments and worked very hard. thankfully, I was able to convince my superiors to transfer me to Lagos. My performance in the first branch I managed earned me the move to a much larger branch within a year. From that branch, I got a bigger offer after a short while. By 2015 (exactly 8 years after I set my crazy goal) I became a deputy general manager, which was just a step lower than planned.

Learn how to set career goals. Where do you see yourself in five years? Remember that your goals must be SMART- Specific, Measurable, Achievable, Realistic and Time-Bound. Your goals must not be ambiguous Get a notebook and write them down.

Be very specific. The goals must not be ambiguous. They must also be measurable. What metrics or parameters will you use to determine whether you're meeting your goals or not? In addition, your goals must be achievable. Some call this "action-oriented". You must be able to execute those goals. You must be ready to break them down into milestones and work them out.

Your goals must also be realistic. Unrealistic goals are useless. Lastly, your goals must be time-bound. This is why nations have yearly budgets and companies have different targets each quarter or year. Give your goal a timeframe.

Writing your goals is important because whatever gets written can get done. Don't just have your goals in your head. Write and keep them in an easily retrievable manner. However, it is not enough to simply write down your goals, and they won't come through by just wishing or praying. You have to act on them. You must run.

Do something daily about the goals that you have written. Don't stay at the same spot. Act. Take a step. Do something about it. Take a corresponding action and see your dreams come true. Also, do not be afraid to review and revise them as you go on.

23

LESSON TWENTYTHREE

FUTURE-PROOF YOUR CAREER

> *"A sensible man watches for problems ahead and prepares to meet them. The simpleton never looks, and suffers the consequences"*
> *- Proverbs 27:12 Living Bible*

It was during the banking consolidation era of Professor Charles Soludo, the then governor of the Central Bank of Nigeria. There were several mergers and acquisitions which led to massive job losses. So many people who had built their careers along a certain path suddenly found out that they could no longer fit into new companies that emerged due to the M&As. In some instances, many were rendered redundant.

I recall how a certain senior manager who had become the zonal head of the audit and compliance team suddenly found himself in another role as the branch head of a marketing unit. He was out of his depth on that role and soon found his exit.

Our world is fast changing. There are jobs that will be different in five years from now or wouldn't exist at all. While I was growing up, there was a high demand for people who could write in shorthand and had good typing skills. At that time, shorthand was a major course in some secretarial institutes. It has all but vanished.

Anyone interested in building a career must consider critically what may likely happen to that company or industry they work for. Will your skill still be relevant over the next five or ten years?

The World Economic Forum anticipates that two-thirds of children starting primary school this year are likely to find themselves taking up jobs that don't even exist today*. According to Oxford University, 47% of jobs will disappear in the next 25 years**.

These postulations are realistic when one considers what has happened over the past few years. In many instances, manual interventions that needed many workers have been replaced by technological innovations.

Less than twenty years ago, many banks used ledgers, passbooks and gave out tally numbers to customers. Clearing a cheque could take as much as a week at that time. But the banking landscape has changed tremendously. It is now online and in real time. It's the same with every sector of the economy.

The traditional career model has also changed. It used to be such that one will specialize in one role, wait through a cycle of promotion and job changes were infrequent. I recall that when I met my father-in-law, the first question he asked was if my job was pensionable. That was the mind-set of that generation. However, the career model that we have known for years has since evolved due to technological advancements, pressure on resources, in addition to cultural and global change.

There is a shift away from the resource-based economy to the knowledge-based and tech-based economy. As a result, some jobs have become extinct and new ones have emerged. About ten years ago, the following jobs were not common or simply did not exist: cloud computing expert, cyber security expert, app developer, Uber driver, blogger, e-business expert, web analyst, social media manager, data miner and so on.

Jobs that will be under threat have these characteristics: low wages, low skill or educational requirements and little creative or social requirements. A cursory look at such roles reveals that this is largely true for typists, post office clerks, file clerks, computer operators, office machine operators, travel agents, retail cashiers, switchboard operators, and the like.

It therefore becomes very critical for anyone who is interested in building a career to learn how to future-proof it. Develop cross-functional skills and have a broad range of competencies, skills and abilities. I usually encourage people to be very adept on their roles but also know a bit about what other people are doing.

Develop skills that you can transfer or take anywhere. Be up to date on your technical skills. Be aware of your environment and also what is happening in your sector globally. Think global. Jobs are being outsourced to other countries and it takes people who are fully prepared to take advantage of such opportunities when they arise.

Learn the use of technologies and collaboration tools within your career. Embrace them and learn how they can help to enhance your job. Work smarter. Build and maintain your professional network. Train and re-train yourself. The future is here.

*World Economic Forum- The Future of Jobs
**Oxford University- The Future of Employment

24

LESSON TWENTY FOUR

HAVE A PLAN B

> *"The best time to start thinking about your retirement is before the boss does"*
> *- Anonymous*

Your career will end one day, regardless of how lucrative it is. You can quit, you can retire, or you can be fired. I've seen exceptional talents being asked to leave and I've had very difficult conversations with staff at various points in my career.

Companies may go through a rough patch and have to right-size in order to stay afloat. Also, mergers and acquisitions happen and staff down-sizing often result. I still can't forget the panic that occurred when a financial institution that I worked for acquired another institution.

It was the year 2005, in the era of banking consolidation in Nigeria, when the capital base of banks was increased to N25b. There were job losses on a massive scale. Families were torn apart when things took a downward turn for their breadwinners. I personally witnessed how it took so many people several years to build their lives all over. Unfortunately, some would never recover.

Anyone who works in a performance-driven environment such as the banking sector in Nigeria understands that a small shift in economic dynamics can make a laggard out of a high-flier. The result can be very brutal.

Losing a job can be very traumatic, especially if one is unprepared. Unfortunately, only a few organizations pay any benefit to affected staff. Forget about gratuity. Such exist only in the public sector and even at that, you may have to wait for several years to get it.

Until a few years ago when the pension act reforms bill took effect and the contributory pension scheme kicked in, very few people who lost their jobs had something to fall back on. Even now, not all members of the private sector participate in the contributory pension scheme.

So essentially, few organizations prepare their staff for a job loss. No training is given and there is no so landing. Many people just find themselves thrust out in the unemployment pool.

Life can happen to anyone and at any time. This is why one must be prepared with a plan B. I usually tell people that I don't have any attachment to any high office or its perks. I only see it as the starting point. I enter my office and I tell myself that someone sat on my seat before me and someone would be on that same seat when I'm gone. Consequently, I do not have any sense of entitlement. Your career is not inheritable.

This makes having a Plan B inevitable. You don't want to be caught napping should your job or career come to an abrupt end. You plan for the rainy day during the dry season. As you start your career, there are at least five different areas that you can take into consideration:

Ideas

Skills

Relationships

Opportunities

Time

Don't neglect ideas that you have. You may be singing on the solution to a challenge faced by your clients. Since every product or service started as an idea, don't ignore yours. An idea clinically executed can guarantee you a lifetime of financial freedom.

Also consider the skills you have. Are there things that you can do better than most people? What are the areas where you have mastery and competence? For me, I decided to utilize my public speaking and writing prowess. As I leveraged upon my strength in these areas, I also discovered that when you play well, people will pay well.

Your career will also bring you across certain relationships. Relationships unlock doors. Don't joke with them. A former managing director of a financial institution once shared the story of how he got a bank licence several years ago. He had built a great relationship with a customer whose account he had managed and much later, the person provided the finance needed to get that licence. That was the secret of his success story.

Value relationships. Look out for opportunities. Take advantage of them and maximize them. Critically consider opportunities in the economy. For instance, the population is an indicator of outstanding opportunities in Nigeria. There are 200 million people who must eat daily, thus there are opportunities in the agricultural sector. There are also areas to explore in retail. We have a budding ICT sector and that is a growth area. You must be passionate and knowledgeable about the area of opportunity that you want to explore.

Finally, you need to figure out what you can do with your time. What do you do what any spare time you have? What can you do on weekends? Can you blog? Can you engage in freelance photography? Can you train? Can you write business proposals or speeches? Can you make beautiful presentations? You can exchange your time for money.

I believe that within these five areas (ideas, skills, relationships, opportunities and time) lies the plan B that anyone can deploy effectively. Live ready. Don't be caught unawares.

However, having such a plan implies that one must have some form of savings. This is why you must learn to put away a certain percentage of your salary as savings. Never spend all you earn. A rule of thumb is to have some months' worth of salary stored away as a buffer. That can be the seed fund for your plan B.

25

LESSON TWENTY FIVE

DON'T POINT THE GUN IF YOU DON'T INTEND TO SHOOT, & OTHER GREAT RULES FOR SUPERVISORS

> *"When you don't keep your word, you lose credibility"*
> *- Robin Sharma*

He that makes promises must keep them. This is why a supervisor should never make a promise flippantly. Reneging on promises will gradually erode your credibility and the less credible you are, the more your leadership authority dwindles. therefore, be known as someone who keeps their words.

If you don't intend to shoot, then don't point the gun. This should hold true irrespective of the nature of the promises, whether good or bad. A promise made should be one kept.

You must also lead by example. Lead from the front. I usually tell my subordinates that I work harder than them all. This is true, and it helps me to demand a greater responsibility from them. Don't demand from your team what you can't do yourself. People will respect you when you show them the way.

Be quick to give your team credit for any good work done. Don't take the glory for the successes recorded in your team. Any team will play selflessly for a coach who doesn't care who takes the credit, as long as they win. However, if they know that the leader would take all the accolades they would never give their best. When new major relationships are initiated, I usually send a mail to my boss praising the relationship officer for the feat. I will never appropriate any achievement that is not mine.

Get involved in the lives of your staff, beyond the office. Staff don't leave organizations; they only leave their supervisors. So be approachable. During a monthly profitability review session with my team in 2013, I gave a relatively new hire feedback about his performance. Suddenly he went into a state of panic. His breathing became laboured and his pupils dilated. I asked him to relax immediately but I knew that something was amiss. His branch manager also whispered to me that the fellow has such attacks during any meeting where his performance is being reviewed.

A few days later, I sent for the man. As he sat down, I asked him to open up to me as I wanted to help. He didn't utter any word. He looked so distressed. Then I asked him if he was epileptic. He nodded. Up till then, he never told anyone about his condition because he was scared that he might lose his job.

I assured him that he could trust me. I got a medical report from him, took it to the head of human resources and made a case for him to be transferred to a less demanding role. When you show your concern for someone, you would command their loyalty for as long as you desire. You can hire competence but you cannot hire loyalty.

Show your staff that you care. Be empathetic. Supervisors must not be so performance-driven that they lose their humanity. At the end of the day, you need people to drive the business.

Little gestures go a long way for your staff too. Remember their birthdays. Get them gifts on their special days. Attend their personal events. You can make such visits a surprise. I remember a particular executive director I once had. He was in town on a business visit when he heard that a very junior member of the team lost his father that morning and wouldn't be coming to work. To the surprise of all, this director asked the branch manager to take him to the staff member's house where he went to pay a condolence visit.

Understand the uniqueness of your staff. No two subordinates are the same. You must therefore understand their strengths, weaknesses and how best they function so that you can deploy their energies appropriately. You get the best out of your team when you deploy people to the area of their strengths. This will also help in the way you relate to the members of your team.

Let your hair down with your staff once in a while. That is one of the ways bonding is achieved. Play with them. Exercise together. Watch a movie together. Be human like the rest of them. Playing together allows them to dispel some myths about you. It would also reveal certain relevant things about their character that you may have never gotten to know.

Periodically allow your team members lead. When you step back, it's an opportunity for your team members to step up. Sometimes, I let a subordinate anchor my meeting while I sit back and observe. It helps them to develop the capacity for leadership and during such times, they can make their mistakes quietly and be corrected.

Communicate with your team frequently. Apart from the monthly sessions I hold, I also send e-mails to staff. To build a high-performing team, effective communication is non-negotiable. Your vision and direction are clearly understood through constant discourse. through communication, you connect with your team and get their buy-in.

Never forget that communication is a two-way thing. It goes beyond mere transmission of information. Communication must flow both ways for it to be effective. Thus, you must actively seek feedback from your team.

26

LESSON TWENTY SIX

BENDING THE RULES MAKE YOU CROOKED

> "Leadership is not a popularity contest"*

A supervisor or a leader is often torn between two situations: to be liked and adored, or to do the right thing. Doing the right thing would often go against the grain.

How does a supervisor handle firing staff? How does one handle giving a poor staff appraisal rating? How does a supervisor handle serving queries or suspension letters without coming off as being high-handed or cruel? I believe that the major key is fairness. Every disciplinary act must be fair and be seen to be so.

There should be no sentiments when it comes to discipline. In fact, I'm usually a bit harder on those I have so spots for. I expect them to play by the rules and even go a bit further. So don't bend the rules for anyone because once you start, you will have to keep bending them for others until you become crooked yourself!

I learnt this lesson sometime in 2010. I had just resumed as the manager in a new branch. However, one of my staff in my previous branch had committed an infraction and I had decided not to escalate the matter because I was trying to help her. At the time, I was not aware but according to our policy, my inaction was an infraction on my part. But even when I finally did the right thing, I was still not spared.

I was issued a query by one of my supervisors who I knew really liked me and who was the one that had given me the opportunity for the new assignment in the first place. In addition to this, I had to serve a two-week suspension, which was recommended by the same supervisor who had just given me a once-in-a-lifetime opportunity role in the new branch. My emotions went riot. I didn't understand why I couldn't get away with a mere slap on the wrist.

My supervisor would later call me for a one-on-one session where she explained why she had to take that step. She knew that the infraction was an error but she said that rules would always be rules. That was professionalism at its best and I came to greatly respect her for the objectivity and fairness.

Supervisors who don't bend the rules are initially disliked and often loathed but on the long run they are respected. As a boss, your goal should be to be right rather than to be popular. Be firm and courageous when taking decisions. Don't be seen as weak as your weakness will make your subordinates resent and exploit you. And don't be a crooked supervisor.

One of my favourite quotes

27

LESSON TWENTY SEVEN

DON'T LOSE YOUR LIFE WHILE CHASING A CAREER

"

Take care of yourself: When you don't sleep, eat crap, don't exercise, and are living off adrenaline for too long, your performance suffers. Your decisions suffer. Your company suffers. Love those close to you: Failure of your company is not failure in life. Failure in your relationship is."

- Ev Williams, co-founder of Medium and Twier

Many people have a career but don't have a life. Unfortunately, such people confuse the two. They work so hard and throw everything into their career that they neglect other necessary things. Their health suffers. Their families suffer, and they do not nurture old relationships. People who can't draw a line and achieve a true work/life balance often have an over-bloated estimation of their self-worth or importance to their company.

The reality of how temporary most things are dawned on me a few years ago. One of the very popular and resourceful branch managers at the organization where I worked was involved in a motor accident and died. We attended his funeral service at Warri and it was right there at the funeral service that I overheard people scheming to take over his role.

The truth is this: work will outlive us. Most times, what the company owes staff in tragic times is just a minute's silence. When the co-founder and managing director of a popular Nigerian bank passed on a few years ago, the bank was not shut down, not even for one day. Business continued as usual.

This is the reason one must create time for family, recreation and periodic medical check-up. Achieving work/life balance can be challenging in certain high-performance environments but proper attention must be paid to it. Spend time with the family especially on weekends and vacations. Go to the cinema and watch movies with them. Take your husband or wife out; eat out sometimes. Go dancing periodically. Do physical exercises and work out together.

Play football with your kids. Make out time for some activities in their schools. My wife and I have an understanding concerning my daughter. I personally take her to school on the first day of every term. Due to the fact that I work out of a location far from my home, I always ensure we do video calls almost every night.

A few years ago, one of my favourite columnists wrote an article about work/life balance. Apparently, the father of the house in the story was used to spending extra hours at work and coming home late. He always got in much later after his daughter was in bed and would leave before she woke up. But he usually joined them for lunch on Sundays and thought that was enough.

On a particular day, however, he had an appointment and couldn't make the Sunday lunch. So his wife sat quietly to eat with her daughter. After a while, the little girl spoke out and asked why 'the man who usually joins them for Sunday lunch' did not show up. The daughter didn't even know that he was her dad!

Don't work too hard that you lose your home or your health. You need a strong body to continue to pursue your career. Without good health, you will find it difficult to move beyond a certain level. Do your annual medical checks. Pay close attention to your blood pressure. I have a blood pressure monitor right beside my bed.

Listen to your body. Once you're fatigued, slow down. You can never be Superman or Superwoman. Don't try to be one. Drink lots of water. It rehydrates and cleanses you. Stay away from addictive drugs. You don't need to ingest any hard substance to deliver extraordinary performance.

Your family needs you more than that career does. You can be replaced at work, but you can't be replaced at home. You are dispensable in the office but indispensable at home. If you lose your career, it's very possible to start all over in another company. But if you lose your health, millions of Naira may not be able to get it back for you. Take care of what is truly important.

LESSON TWENTY EIGHT

REMEMBER TO HAVE FUN AT WORK

> *"People rarely succeed unless they have fun in what they are doing"*
> **-Dale Carnegie**

There was a month when the performance of my team was outstanding, and I brought a deejay to the monthly performance review session. The guy introduced the presenters with hit songs and scratched the turntable at significant moments during the presentations. And that was not the only time that I brought a DJ to the office.

I've even brought a traditional drummer to work. I've organized retreat sessions for my team where we had parties, took part in bonding activities, had a singing competition, swum, ate barbecue and had invited inspirational speakers to motivate us.

I can still recall an awards night that we planned. There were many categories that the staff voted on: from best dressed to friendliest staff, best team of the year, and so many others. We first held a notable daily countdown where staff were treated to several teasers as the weekend event approached. Then the day came and the programme was held at a resort far away from the branches. Plaques and trophies were presented to winners and there was a red-carpet ceremony, which was so colourful that the memory lingers.

Imagine hosting more than a hundred people over a weekend of fun! I recall that I held a similar weekend session in one of the banks where I worked and invited the managing director, who after attending mandated the other regions to hold similar events. The result was that there was a marked improvement in performance.

If you work at a typical job, you'll spend around a minimum of 8 hours daily at work but if it's a job like mine, it's around 12 hours or even more, which comes to about 60 hours per week. This means that I spend more time with my colleagues at work than I spend with my family. Also, if you go by the average number of productive years of a person, you will spend at least a third of your entire life at work. This is why as much as is practicable, it's important to create an atmosphere of fun at work.

Another thing that you can do is to take your meetings away from the office. There was a time I held my weekly meeting with my team at a popular Thai restaurant. When I sent out the notice of the meeting, some of my team members called to be sure that it was not an error! It was such a different feeling as we held our meeting over sumptuous breakfast. When I visit upcountry locations, I take my time to bond with the team over fish barbecue and drinks after work. It's interesting having everyone let down their guard and loosening up. You can actually see people being real when they're having fun. Your team will trust you more and relate with you better.

Fun makes people more committed as they often want to repeat the experience, especially if you make it clear that you will hold such sessions more often if productivity improves or certain targets are met. So be creative but work within your office policies and guidelines. Do not forget that it is still work, after all! And you may need to carry your HR department along to ensure that you don't flout any rule.

Have fun at work. It pays!

29

LESSON TWENTY NINE

YOUR BEST RETIREMENT PLANS ARE THE PEOPLE YOU BUILD

> *You may go wrong on other investments but you can never go wrong on investing in people.*

It was indeed a very humbling experience as it slowly dawned on me. Seated right with me at the regional session were three people who had been my subordinates (relationship officers), and on my recommendation had become branch managers like me. I am happy that reproducing myself has been the trend in the course of my career. Even as a regional head, I have produced another regional head.

The greatest legacy any supervisor or leader can leave in an organization is to produce other leaders. Leaders should breed leaders. Building capacity in others ensures that we have core staff who are able to handle tasks and assignments with minimal supervision.

The true success of a leader is not the percentage of sales targets or profitability budgets met. Lasting success is not measured by annual revenue or income. If you measure success only this way, you're wrong because success is a moving target. The targets of this year will be obsolete by next year. True and lasting success is measured by the number of people whose capacity you have stretched beyond when they first met you.

This is why a critical task for a supervisor is coaching and mentoring staff. Over the last couple of years, I've had a board and flip chart in my office which I use to teach those who report to me. I don't wait for them to be sent on official training. Rather, I commit time to personally guide them. After all, the better they are, the easier the work becomes, even for me.

So, when they bring memos for me to approve or sign, I usually spend some time educating them about the subject matter. I realize that my workforce is a reflection of me and I can never be better than the sum total of the staff who report to me. e more highly skilled they are, the better our output as a team. You're only as good as the weakest link within your team.

Thus, the true effectiveness of a leader is the ability of his people to continue and handle tasks successfully in his absence. If you're on vacation and still have to check your mails and intervene regularly even when you have someone sitting in for you, then you have failed to develop capacity in your team.

Give your team members wings to fly. Allow them to learn from their failures and mistakes. Delegate, but don't micro-manage except it is absolutely necessary. Nurture them. Correct them. Teach them. Encourage them. Discipline them. The stronger each of them becomes individually, the stronger the whole team gets. We rise by lifting each other, so the leader will also rise each time the subordinates rise.

This should be your focus if you don't want your name to be forgotten as soon as you exit that office. Don't be only interested in having monuments. If you build your people, then they will build monuments in addition to building the balance sheet. Your retirement plan should thus not consist only in the savings you put away or the various investments you have made.

Your greatest retirement plan should be people. That's an investment that will pay lasting dividends in lasting satisfaction and internal fulfilment. You may go wrong with other investments but not with your people. That's how to leave a legacy.

30

LESSON THIRTY

FIND MEANING OUTSIDE YOUR CAREER

> *Remember that a job, even a great job or a fantastic career, doesn't give your life meaning, at least not by itself. Life is about what you learn, who you are or can become, who you love and are loved by.*
> **- Fran Dorf, Author and Psychotherapist**

Your life should not solely be defined by your career. If career is all there is to you then your life will lack its desired impact and true meaning. If your job defines you then the day you lose your job or retire may very well be the day that you lose the essence of life. Your career is not who you are.

While your occupation may put food on the table and pay the bills, there is
more to you than that. You're more than that 8 to 5. You're more than just
attending to customers and wearing a big smile. You're more than your pay package, no matter how huge it is.

Most leaders that we know make an effort to look for meaning outside their career. They get involved in causes that are bigger than them and are not only about profit. They use the knowledge and influence obtained from their careers to advance life's higher callings. They understand that life goes beyond the abundance of things a man possesses.

This is the reason that men like Bill Gates, Warren Buffet, Tony Elumelu and others are involved in social entrepreneurship. They set up foundations or get involved in one charitable cause or the other.

If all you live for is to get to the peak of your profession, then your joy will be lost by the time you attain that feat. There is a difference between a good life and a great life. You can achieve a good life within your career, with all the attendant perks of office and pleasure that come with it. However, achieving a great life beyond the confines of your career requires transcendence. It involves expanding the scope of your influence.

Over the course of my career, I've had several opportunities to get involved in social causes and interventions. It is when you get involved that you will understand that there is no greater satisfaction than watching the lives of people or your society being transformed. Having money or wealth alone can never give you that satisfaction.

There is a public school in Ibadan that I adopted. I provided the school with playground equipment and repaired the borehole that gives water to the community where the school is based. When I realized that only about 2 out of the 25 enrolled children had uniforms, I provided them with new ones. I have given out exercise books and paid common entrance fees. In addition, every Christmas period since 2016, I have made sure that there is a Santa

Claus grotto at the school.

In 2017, I was involved in an intervention where I raised the sum of eight hundred and seventy thousand Naira (N870,000) via friends on social media towards the payment of fines for 27 prison inmates at the Kirikiri medium prisons in Lagos. I worked in conjunction with a music artiste and humanitarian, Lamboginny. Nothing can describe the joy of seeing those former inmates take a walk into freedom.

My alma mater had been closed for about a year, due to a protracted crisis and I was saddened about it. Therefore I decided to call on four friends of mine who were also alumni of the institution. After a serious brainstorming exercise, #FundLautech was born.

As chief initiator, I would lead this team across several states, giving radio talks and raising funds for the institution. We engaged celebrities to endorse our efforts, composed jingles, interacted with kings and several notable individuals, used social media to advance our efforts, and generally brought a serious national awareness to what was previously a local issue.

Over a period of 90 days in 2017 we raised the sum of nine million and four hundred thousand Naira (N9,400,000), which we handed over to the university in a very transparent manner. The names of all donors were reflected openly on our website and we didn't take a dime for our efforts. In fact, all accruing expenses were from our own pockets.

But the greatest joy for me came from knowing that many undergraduate students benefited from the vocational training offered by various companies who had partnered with our #FundLautech initiative during the closure.

I've not written the above examples out of self-glorification. It is simply to challenge every career person that the true measure of our lives is in our donations. We can all change the world around us a person at a time.

You can pay someone's school fees. You can volunteer to teach at a local school periodically. You can control traffic on your street. You can mobilize people to fill potholes on your road. You can start a foundation that will cater to an underserved segment. You don't have to be extremely rich to start. All you need is to be resourceful.

By doing this, your life will be more meaningful, and that's when you truly start to live.

PERSONAL NOTES

A LETTER FROM MY MENTOR

The mail was sent to me on March 23, 2003. A few months prior, I had left the first financial organization that I worked for. However, I was in a fix as my previous employer wanted me back. I was also frustrated at the new office due to some internal policies that I found restrictive. Going back to the previous comfort zone looked very attractive and I was willing to, even on my old grade. But I had the good sense of sending a mail to my mentor explaining my dilemma and seeking counsel. He is a consummate professional of many years standing and I had approached him to mentor me when I started my career.

His response is included below. I've removed the names of affected organizations and individuals, but the letter is reproduced unedited with consent from my mentor.

Dear Bayo,

I feel you should not go back to ---------- Bank. You should not return from where you have already left. I was not especially keen on your going to ---------- bank for all I had heard about the way ------------- operates. I do not know him but I have heard about his style from a friend who works at ------------------.

Going back to ---------Bank increases the risk of bad blood. Those who do not want you (not you as a person but people who your progress will slow down or deny opportunity) will remember you for having left the bank in the first place. You do not need all this. They are asking you to accept your old grade? They do not want you badly enough. Forget about the appreciation bit. It is good to be appreciated. However, like I have heard today in a preaching by TD Jakes, do not expect appreciation from the workplace. It leads to frustration and confuses clear thinking. The guy who wants you needs you for now to get the job done. If David shines more than Saul tomorrow, he will throw javelins at David. You have God-given skills. God will provide a way for them to provide for your family and for them to be better used elsewhere as He may indicate to you.

If you become dissatisfied with -----------, God can send you a signal to move on. I am not comfortable with you going back to -------Bank (even though I did not really want you to leave earlier). Take your chances with your God. Perhaps you are anointed to work with ----------. TD Jakes did mention (and it made sense to me that is why I repeat it) that evil can also come to manifest the talent and the anointing of God. The Spirit of God left Saul and was replaced by an evil spirit "from the Lord". All things worked together to bring David into Saul's palace. It was not the best of working environments but it was more honourable and there was no talk of returning to mend the sheep.

However, do talk to my wife. She has been in the banking industry and is also aware of these politics. She will be very happy to talk to you. You can tell her of my position after you have listened to hers.

I do not think you should return to --------Bank because you have left. Let it be the Lord Himself who will talk to you clearly if you are to go against it. His is the last word. I have declared my opinion.

God bless. Relax though. Forget about all the appreciation bit. You should know human beings. They are dangerous. You need better reasons than that. It is not only about money. Even if they offered you the same salary, my opinion will not change. The appreciation and interest in you has come too late. David has moved to Saul's court. Not that Saul's court is not without its dangers, but David has moved on. Only be like David. Be thou convinced by what you decided with God when you were leaving. Do not look left or right.

Let me stop. I want you to have time to think it over and I do not want to be too overbearing on you. Show your wife what I wrote. God will help you take the best decision.

AG

Last word: I listened to his counsel and stayed where I was. In a few months, I got another offer from yet another institution with a promotion. If I hadn't obeyed his counsel, I would have gone back to my comfort zone on my previous grade and who knows how that would have impacted my career. This underscores the importance of mentoring.

Get a mentor today.

AN UNFORGETTABLE TEAM*

I called the meeting to appreciate my Southwest 1 Team. I wanted to appreciate them as I formally exited the organization. It was meant to be a day of cocktails and small chops but my staff turned it around and planned a coup for me. It became a day of tributes and celebration. There was a DJ on standby who dished out great songs intermittently. I listened almost with tears in my eyes as my team spoke about me. I had no idea that we had forged such a strong bond in such a short time.

During the 'small chops' break we had, I stood aside drinking my chapman. Then a young chap I had never seen approached me. He almost prostrated as he told me his story. He had been sacked for poor performance just before I took over the region. I went on a business call with his branch manager to a certain customer and his issue came up. Obviously, he was well known to the customer and the customer wasn't happy that such a diligent staff was fired. I promised to investigate and do something about it. Everyone I spoke to testified to how hardworking he was. Everyone had something good to say about him. Eventually, I found out that he was actually posted to a wrong location. He was simply a good staff in wrong geography! I recalled him and posted him to a place that he was familiar with. I didn't even know him personally and I didn't see him until that day.

Another staff of mine got me a gift and shared how I calmed her fears a few weeks before. She came from the doctor's office straight to my office and needed to talk. I saw she was worried and offered her a seat. She was due for a minor invasive surgery called a laparoscopy. I told her that my wife once had one and took time to explain to her that she didn't have to worry. I honestly didn't know that my encouragement lifted her spirit. She thanked me profusely and prayed for me. For me, banking has gone beyond being a career and is now a ministry of sorts.

I took time out to appreciate my branch managers for supporting me. I presented to each of them a copy of Malcolm Gladwell's book, David & Goliath. I also appreciated one of the contract staff by giving her a personal cash donation. She had distinguished herself by initiating a very significant relationship. I also paid tribute to my Secretary, Irene. Believe me, Irene is the best secretary in the world. She works for very long hours and never complains. Whenever I worked late, Irene would stay in the office with me till 10pm at times and have to be escorted home by a security guard. She would take minutes very diligently and ensure I got all my reports in a timely manner. Irene understood exactly how I want my coffee. She knew when to interrupt and when not to. She played a perfect host for my guests. She was absolutely loyal to a fault. In all the time I worked with her, I never lifted my voice against her.

However, my team was set to out-do me as they also presented a gift to me. We took to the dance floor and grooved. I personally requested for 'Ijo Shina' by Shina Peters. The whole place erupted as we took to the floor. I laughed as I watched my staff danced 'Sekem'. I did some tap dancing with Fred Rabiu as the DJ blared Pharell Williams' 'Happy'. I pulled my Secretary, Irene to the dancing floor as Olamide's 'Awon goons mi' played. In between, Eniola Jegede was an outstanding compere. One of the best highlights of the day for me was when he sang 'O ti mu mi gbagbe o, Ibanuje igba kan' (God has caused me to forget the sorrows of yesterday). It was so moving as everyone joined and sang at the top of their voices. It is a day I will never forget in my life.

Earlier in the day, I had sent out this mail below to all my staff. An abridged version is reproduced below:

My dear South West 1 Team,

This is a very emotional moment for me as I know goodbyes are not easy. I want to take this time out to sincerely appreciate each and every one for your support during my brief sojourn leading the team. I call it a sojourn because life is a journey and never a destination. We will all never 'arrive' in the real sense of it and people must move on at certain periods in their lives. That is exactly what I'm doing. You've all been part of my life just like I have been part of yours. I'm particularly delighted and it is my sincere joy to note that together, we have made some progress. We are not exactly where we want to be but then we are no longer where we were when I assumed leadership of this Region a short while ago.

So, let me leave you with a few 'take-aways' as I take my bow:

1. MYTHS ARE MEANT TO BE SHATTERED

When I resumed in the Southwest, the fashionable reason for the poor performance was the excuse that the state governments were owing salaries. It had become so endemic and had assumed the proportion of a myth that people had grown to believe it to be true. It took a carefully contrived business plan showing that we were sitting on a gold mine of opportunities for the myth to be shattered.

What are the myths that are still affecting your performance? Your location? Your staffing? Your vehicles? Shatter the myths. Break the jinx. Think outside the box. No, throw away the box. Be creative. Have a paradigm shift. Your performance is a product of your ability to think and be creative. Limitations and barriers have to be broken in your mind before you can conquer them physically. Stop making up excuses for poor performance. There may be forty million reasons for failure but there's not a single excuse (Rudyard Kipling). Excuses are the nails used to build a house of failure.

2. NO ONE HAS BAD STAFF-JUST POOR LEADERSHIP

Up till now, I have not recruited a single staff since I assumed leadership here. I have worked practically with all the people I met on ground. I didn't change or remove any branch manager except for those who are on recovery suspension. Yes, there are times when it is necessary to move people around especially when they have been on that role for some time as this prevents the law of diminishing returns from setting in and also offers the staff a new challenge. I also need to balance this out. Some staff by their attitude and laziness condemn themselves to a situation where they become irrelevant and useless to the ideals of the organization. Such must of a necessity be shown the door.

However, I'm of the opinion that when people usually complain about their staff, often times, you actually need to check the quality of their leadership. A bad workman complains of his tools. A staff is a reflection of the leader- either for good or for bad. A leader's job is to work on their staff in order to improve the quality and also affect the quantum of output. A great leader will invest time and efforts in developing his team. The better your team are, the easier for the leader.

That's the reason I started the Thursday trainings. I hope this can be continued and sustained.

3. YOU CAN'T GIVE WHAT YOU DON'T HAVE

A ball bounces and rises not only because of the kick to the ball but because of the inflated air pressure within the ball. That is why a deflated ball is useless. Personal development is key. Don't wait for the bank to train you- train yourself. You owe it to yourself to continue to develop your capacity and capabilities. I usually tell people that my life is a summary of two things: the people I've met and the books I've read. So I make it a duty to work on my mind. I absorb so much information and knowledge so I can exhale the right contribution. That's what you must do consistently. Read. There are so many good books around. Invest on your mind. Reading affects the quality of your thoughts and impact on the way you communicate. The phone you carry is a veritable source of great information. Use it wisely- not just on browsing entertainment but for improving the quality of your output.

4. THINK OF HOW YOU CAN ADD VALUE

A few days ago, during my visit to Osogbo, one of the team members complained about how difficult the banking terrain has now become- especially with the recent developments such as the Treasury Single Account (TSA), inability to lodge cash deposits into domiciliary accounts, irregularity of salary payments to public sector workers among others. My response to her was that for anyone to survive and be outstanding during this period, we must begin to think of how to add value to our customers. The days are gone when you will just go cap in hand begging for deposits!

What value can you add to a customer? How can you make a customer's business better? How can you make your client more profitable? What's your value proposition? Can you help them become more efficient thereby saving them some money? Can you introduce a new line of business to them so as to diversify their portfolio and spread their risks? Can you give them timely financial advice so they can prepare ahead?

Recently, I was introduced to a customer that has almost completed a 60-room boutique hotel in a very upscale location. She had built the hotel absolutely debt-free. So many banks were on her for the new business. The good news is that she has given our bank 100% of the business and signed up for our POS. Do you want to know how? I discovered she knew next to nothing about social media marketing and I suggested advertising her hotel on hotels.ng and Jovago. I also registered a website domain name for the hotel at a personal cost of 5k. Two things will separate the boys from the men now—and that is excellent service and the value you can add.

5. THE MAJOR CURRENCY FOR TRANSACTIONS IS NOT MONEY-IT'S INTEGRITY

That's an area we must focus on in the Southwest. There's the need to change the perception of the region. Attention must be given to honesty in all we do. With integrity, you have nothing to fear since you have nothing to hide. Don't take a short cut as you will end up cutting short your destiny. Good things will eventually come to those who wait. Don't have excess of everything and be deficit in integrity.

Honesty still remains the very best policy. A life of integrity opens doors- even long after you're gone. Don't cut deals. Life has a way of rewarding everything that has been done-whether good or life of integrity opens doors- even long after you're gone. Live above board and try your best to make your life and dealings transparent.

To everyone I've worked with- Victoria Island Region, Ikeja Region and now Southwest 1 Region, I remain grateful for the time we spent together. May God be with you till we meet again.

Adebayo Adeyinka

* This article is based on a mail I sent to my team members on Nov 11, 2015. It was my last day at that organization.

My Victoria Island Team:

4 LEADERSHIP LESSONS & GREAT MEMORIES*

Uche had been calling me for more than a week asking when I would come to Victoria Island. I knew certainly that she must be up to something. Yesterday, I decided to go and I sent her a text that I was on my way. As I entered her office which was in the same location as what used to be my office, I was pleasantly shocked at what I saw behind her desk.

My former team had a big surprise for me. I call them former now reluctantly because I had just moved to another role about a month ago. As Uche hugged me and presented the gift of a 47-inch JVC Smart LED TV, words failed me to express how much I appreciated the best team in the whole world. All I could just utter was 'thank you'. Yes, my team has given me several gifts in the past—a bedside refrigerator, a suit, lovely Italian and pure leather shoes, belt, numerous cakes, wall frames, cards and so many others (a team member even brought a live turkey to my house once and that kept my daughter busy. I can remember Kiki shouting, "Daddy, the turkey has pooed. Come and clean her bum bum"). I thought this gift was just too much.

Since yesterday, I've reflected on our journey of over 3 years: How we have rubbed off on each other, the pains, the joys, the sacrifices made, the often unpalatable decisions I had to take as a leader, the successes we recorded, our failures, and leadership lessons this great team taught me. I felt the best appreciation and tribute I can pay to this amazing team was to put down some of my leadership reflections and share some of the memories that will linger for the rest of my life:

1. THE PEOPLE YOU FOCUS ON WILL DELIVER THE RESULTS YOU WANT

When I took on the role in 2012, I took one look at my team and made up my mind people would come first. I knew that was the only way to guarantee a lasting success. The people you build will build the business you want. According to Ken Goldstein, it is "people first. Then products. And then profits. In that order". And that is my philosophy.

I spent my time training and focusing on their personal development. At a point, I bought a white board in my office and started a Thursday Training Session for all my team members. I made it compulsory for every sales person to attend the weekly training which spanned two hours. I poured out my heart at those sessions. I taught about 30 people weekly as I shared from my experience. The bank didn't ask me to conduct the sessions neither was I paid for them. I taught them about letters of credit, The 5Cs of Credit (now 7Cs), the different types of credit facilities, how to evaluate a credit proposal, the different types of collateral security, credit documentation, how to sell to customers, the art of relationship management and many other topics.

My team asked me questions and put me on my toes. I spiced each training session with real stories. I know people learn better when you share stories- Jesus always used that format as most of his teachings were in parables. What they didn't know was that each session took me hours to prepare. I read widely and encouraged them to do so.

Sometimes in June 2012, I decided to take my team to an off-site retreat. I set up a committee to identify a location and work out the modalities. The retreat was to cost us a very princely sum in six figures but I encouraged my team to buy in and I levied each team member including myself based on grade and level. We raised a significant amount and I approached my former Executive Director who graciously donated the balance. And so off we went to Hermitage Resort, Akodo (around Lekki Free Trade Zone) for 2 days (the whole of Saturday and Sunday morning) of bonding.

I didn't allow anyone to take their personal car. Everyone parked in VI and took the 2 buses I already booked. No one was allowed to leave the venue until we finished on Sunday morning. We played, I jumped into the swimming pool with my team, we played beach football and had a beach party on Saturday night as we brought a DJ who played great music from Shina Peters (E ja wo lapon ti o yo, e lo gbomi ila ka na, Shina gbode) to PSquare. We had buffet for each meal- breakfast, lunch and dinner.

I invited my friend Paago Aleele who delivered an inspirational talk. At the end of Paago's talk, we all held each other and sang R Kelly's "I believe I Can Fly". I invited my former Managing Director who was present during the talk and he also encouraged us. Of course, we also had a strategy and performance session.

Needless to say, the performance of my team went up significantly after the event. Branches that had been on red turned black. A particular branch that had almost been written off because of a preponderance of huge non-performing assets turned the corner and started delivering notable profits- despite the presence of the NPLs. My team members went into over-drive. Energy levels soared. Management took notice and the former MD directed other Regions to hold similar retreat sessions. In 2012, our profit increased by over 300% compared to the previous year.

In 2013, my team members clamoured for a similar retreat. This time, we chose the Peninsular Resort at Sangotedo, Ajah. I invited Nath McAbraham-Inajoh who spoke to us about "The Winning Mindset". I remember our DJ almost marred the event as he came very late but we still had a great time. The food was good and the drinks were plenty. We invited some other Unit Heads and external facilitators who made presentations. That year, our profit increased by almost 120% compared to the previous year.

A leader's job is about building the people. The people you build will build the results you want. If you care about your team, they will also care about you. People don't leave organizations- they leave their leaders. I always boastfully say that even when my team members leave the company we work for, they never leave me. I have come to understand that there is a greater retirement benefit than money- and that is people.

2. PEOPLE BUY INTO YOU FIRST BEFORE THEY BUY INTO YOUR VISION

At the first retreat session we held, I unveiled our vision for the Region. I heard so many people gasp as I said we will end up being a case study at the Lagos Business School. I asked my team to stand up as we recited the vision over and over again. It was quite ambitious but for me, nothing less will ever do.

However, I realized people will buy into the leader first before they buy into their vision. So I had set out early to connect emotionally first. People think emotionally before they are logical. You have to connect to their hearts before you can connect to their heads. I knew everyone by name. I took more than a passing interest in people. I understood that people don't care how much you know until they know how much you care. I engaged in chit-chat with everyone occasionally. I sat with my officers at their desks. I bought books for some. I took a few for lunch. Some discussed very personal issues with me.

I remember a team member who had cancer shortly before I joined. He came to my office to narrate his experience and I almost wept as he showed me the bag he was carrying under his suit. I knew he couldn't withstand the rigour and pressure of sales and marketing and I knew he needed the job so he could pay for his medication. I took the case up personally, liaised with HR and my Line ED and ensured he got another role that was less demanding. We were very close colleagues until he breathed his last.

I complimented team members' hair-do and dressing. I gave a few nick-names. I exchanged banter with many. I made myself accessible to all. My door was always open. If I was in the office, you didn't have to drop anything with my Secretary- I would take a look and sign off right away. I responded to my e-mails promptly. If your people know you always read your mails, they will read theirs also. I came early for meetings and my team members knew they couldn't come late. I challenged my Managers to lead by example- I already set the standard. There was the need to make myself believable and likeable and I think I was able to achieve that largely.

So it became easy for my team members to buy into our vision when I unveiled it. I had people working for me even when they were working for the organization. They knew they couldn't afford to disappoint me. It had become a personal thing. Did we achieve our vision? The jury is still out.

3. REWARD SWIFTLY BUT PUNISH SLOWLY

Leaders must celebrate the achievements and successes of their team members, no matter how little. This is especially more so when a team is trying to find its feet. Every milestone achieved counts. In the early days of our team, I started the habit of celebrating every achievement by sending a "well done" mail to the team member and copying both his/her manager and our ED. When the achievement is significant, I even copied the MD. I encouraged each member to share their success with me. Most leaders don't know how their team members value their compliments! Mark Twain wrote that he could live on a compliment a day.

I also gave out personal rewards to celebrate achievements. Some little cash here and there, especially to contract staff. I recognized good performance openly. During our monthly meetings, I usually ask the team member involved to share his/her experience so we can learn from it and then we all give the person an ovation. I always celebrated my team openly by calling them the best team in the bank. I said that at every opportunity I got.

But then I also punished issues of integrity hard and fast. I put down attitude issues very promptly. However, I'm slow and calculating on issues of performance. I know almost anyone will thrive under the right conditions. I also consider how hard and cold it is for someone to be unemployed. I believe everyone deserves a second chance.

Talking about second chances, I remember the case of a female team member who got fired. She got on my case and never gave up. For almost 3 months, she still came to the office daily, sent me numerous texts pleading for another chance and just about harassed me to a point of submission. I had never seen such perseverance in my entire life. I knew there must be something more to this lady. So I re-hired her on the same level she was exited. I redeployed her to another branch entirely and she had to start afresh. The day she resumed for the second time, I called her to my office and she promised to shock me. Yes, she did shock me with her performance. She was so outstanding that I had no choice but to promote her and she ended up being the best staff I had in that region. She managed the number 1 account we had in the entire region! She will certainly read this note as she's not only my Facebook friend but she's now my personal friend.

So I mentor laggards and even move them around, so I can get the best out of them. If I have to let you go (and I did fire a few), then it means your case is almost beyond redemption.

4. LEADERS MUST PRODUCE OTHER LEADERS AND NOT JUST FOLLOWERS

I pride myself in the fact that at a point, I could go on vacation and handover to any of the 7 Managers I had. Each one of them could act for me and I wouldn't bat an eyelid. They had raised their capacity to such an extent that I could delegate freely without fear. I had no fear that anyone would take my seat- I even encouraged them to do so. There was a day I told them I was tired of the role and I wanted one of them to grab my seat. There were times I had them anchor meetings where I was present and my contributions were very sparse.

I allowed them to make their own mistakes and learn from them. Instead of being the lone star, I was happy to have additional 7 stars in the team. I encouraged them to make presentations- even when the MD was present and everyone would have thought I should make those presentations. I only interjected once in a while during such presentations.

I am exceedingly happy that I reproduced myself by producing another regional head (he was one of my managers) from my team. I was too eager to rub it in during management sessions that he was my product. Before I left the previous organization I worked for, I produced three branch managers among my team members from the branch I headed. When I sat with them at meetings of branch managers, I usually felt a tinge of satisfaction within me. I gauge my success not just from the profits made but from the leaders I raise.

I have such great memories of our time together. We had our fights and my MPR Sessions made even the bold to cringe. I remember some team members would have paid not to attend some sessions-especially if they were not doing well. I would have sent a mail earlier that attendance was mandatory and nobody was allowed to fall sick. I remember I told my team members that headache is not a disease and it's only a condition. I told them malaria does not kill Africans so nobody should tell me he or she has malaria. I pushed them hard and I had to work harder to keep up pace with my team. In over 3 years (since 2012 till date), I only missed work once and that is recently when I had to take a day off when I became ill obviously from stress.

I have not been perfect but I'm striving hard for it. Excellence is a moving target. I don't assume that everyone likes me but leadership is not a popularity contest. I'd rather be right than be popular. I took some hard decisions but I was left with no choice. I made some mistakes but I'm better off now as I learnt from them. You guys made the team worth leading. You gave me the opportunity to lead you and you submitted to my leadership. For that, I'm grateful. To all past and present team mates, I hope I inspired you to be the best you can be.

Uche, Wale, Maria, my own Ijeoma, Mary, Eunice and Christy and everyone in your teams and branches both former and present (I can't mention all of you by name), may God bless you for this gift. May you be greater than me in Jesus Name.

*This article was written on August 8, 2015 after my team gave me a wonderful gift- a 47-inches JVC Smart LED TV- on my transfer to another location.

HOW TO CREATE YOUR WORLD IN SEVEN DAYS*

Dear Team,

It's been my first week with the team and what a week it has been. We had a fantastic strategy session and people gave commitments with boldness. And some are making it good already.

But quite a number are nowhere near their commitments. Fortunately, there is still one more week to go. What is the value of one week? What can be done in one week?

In one week, God created the heaven and the earth and all that is in it- including man. That's huge. The stars, the moon, the sun, trees, all the animals, the various type of fishes, flora and fauna in one week and even took a day off to rest. How did He do it? I think I have an idea.

1. He did something every day. He didn't do everything at once. Make each day count and don't just count the days. Do something that makes you get closer to your targets. Break it down to achievable bits.

2. Focus.
Don't run around without a plan. Strategy is better than energy. Avoid distractions. Always have the goal in mind.

3. Review

On a daily basis, God stepped back to review what He did and it was good. Review. Your daily reports from your team. Don't gloss over any information.

4. Team work

God said, "Let us make". It is "us" and not "I". A team will always do better than an individual. Leverage on one another. Go out on calls in twos. Don't allow anyone to visit a customer alone. What one forgets, another may remember.

As you take your rest this weekend, remember that you can meet your commitments in one week. You can create your own world in seven days.

Happy weekend.

*Excerpts of a mail I sent to my staff on Jan 23, 2016 when I just joined the team.

CAREER
30 LESSONS
I LEARNT ALONG THE WAY

If you are interested in starting or ramping up your career, then this book is for you! The author uses intensely personal experiences and real-life examples to reveal what you need to know about:

* When and how to position yourself for a job change,
* How to ace your next interview,
* The dynamics of emotional intelligence and being street-smart,
* How to be a great supervisor or manager,
* Rules for managing office politics and superiors, and much more.

This book also contains timely secrets that will make your career future-proof. In addition, you will discover how to avoid the numerous pitfalls that can put a drag on your career.

BAYO ADEYINKA

Bayo Adeyinka had his first degree in engineering but has worked in the financial sector for almost twenty years, where he has led a remarkable career in commercial and retail banking. Apart from holding an MBA, he is a fellow and honorary member of many professional institutes.
He loves mentoring and training others and has spearheaded many notable charitable causes. He is also a published author with 2 books to his credit and several articles which have appeared in major newspapers and gone viral on social media.

Inspirational, Motivational

Cover Design: Dayo Okeowo

www.ingramcontent.com/pod-product-compliance
Lightning Source LLC
Chambersburg PA
CBHW030648220526
45463CB00005B/1679